SUPER CHEAP JAPAN

Budget Travel in Tokyo, Kyoto, Osaka, Nara, Hiroshima and Surrounding Areas

Matthew Baxter

Help spread the word!

Please help us by writing a review on the website where you bought the book, sharing the book on Facebook or Twitter, or telling a friend. As this is a self-funded indie project, it would be super useful and very much appreciated! Arigatou!

Like or follow us to get the latest tips and deals

Join us on Facebook at https://www.facebook.com/supercheapjapan or follow us on Twitter at https://twitter.com/SuperCheapJapan to receive information on new discounts, latest deals and interesting budget travel reports. You can also join our newsletter for monthly roundups of this information at http://www.supercheapjapan.com/.

Super Cheap Japan
9 Eashing Lane
Godalming, Surrey GU7 2JZ
www.supercheapjapan.com/contact/

Book Layout ©2017 BookDesignTemplates.com

Ordering Information:
Special discounts are available on quantity purchases by corporations, associations, and others. For details, contact the "Special Sales Department" at the address above.

Super Cheap Japan: Budget Travel in Tokyo, Kyoto, Osaka, Nara, Hiroshima and Surrounding Areas / Matthew Baxter - 1st ed.
Paperback ISBN 978-1-9998100-0-9
Ebook ISBN 978-1-9998100-1-6

Contents

Welcome to Japan

View over Shinjuku, to Mount Fuji

Welcome to the Land of the Rising Sun, but with this book not the land of rising prices! Japan is a fascinating country, but unfortunately one with a reputation for being expensive. This has been changing rapidly over the last few years, with increasingly good exchange rates for foreigners and tax-free shopping galore, among other things. This guide is here to help you save as much as possible, and in the end have a much better holiday. We will show you how to experience the highlights of Honshu, Japan's main island, without burning a hole in your pocket. This includes the popular tourist hotspots of Tokyo, Kyoto, Nara, Osaka and Hiroshima, as well as many nearby tourist spots to keep your trip varied and as exciting as possible.

Highlights of Japan map

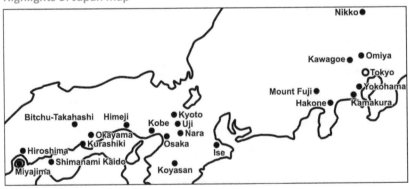

Japan is a deeply historic and traditional culture, yet one that is also very modern and at times futuristic. This mix is what makes the country stand out from the rest. One minute you will be soaking in a hot spring bath, another playing with a talking robot and another inside a 1000-year-old shrine. What sets Japan apart from other countries is its extensive, easy to use train and bus networks, which budget travelers can use to explore many places, while easily keeping an eye on their budget. From the deeply spiritual to the plain crazy, Japan has it all.

Popular meals include gyudon (beef on rice with a mild, sweet sauce), tempura (deep fried food), yakisoba (fried noodles) and ramen (noodles in a thick broth). These can be found with prices starting from just a few dollars, and are available almost everywhere. Convenience stores, which you'll usually never be a few minutes away from, also have these items, plus cheap drinks and snacks. Many hostels also offer free drinks, snacks and bike rentals to entice guests to stay with them.

Japan can seem like another world, and has developed a very unique and at times fascinating culture. It's a very safe society, one where drinking outside on the streets will never cause you any trouble and where people always return lost items they have found. Japanese people are generally very welcoming for foreign tourists, and while their English skills can present problems, people really try their best to help. Don't be surprised if you ask a shop owner for directions to your hostel and they close the shop to guide you there personally, or offer to give you a ride for free!

The increasingly favorable exchange rate has made Japan much more affordable compared to before. A ramen meal would have cost about $9 in 2012, but it now costs $5.50, while an average hostel room used to cost around $40, but now comes in at $24. These kinds of prices have helped Japan to increase tourism numbers significantly. While this does mean that the top spots are becoming rather crowded, there have been many benefits, such as improved English language support, countless new discount train passes, extensive free wifi coverage and more frequent transportation services in the countryside. Your timing could not be better for a budget trip to the Land of the Rising Sun.

How to save on your holiday with this book

This book is very different from the rest, and the emphasis is on traveling on a budget. Here are some tips on how to use the book to save you as much as possible.

Itineraries

For each region, and nationally, use the sample itineraries based on train or bus passes to help you plan your budget trip. The best way to save is to base your trip around these passes, connecting between them with a cheap bus or short train ride if needed. You'll save a bunch, as train passes can save you hundreds of dollars, or thousands if in a group!

Things to do

Look out for places listed as FREE, or with free sample or discounts available. Try doing the free ones that interest you first, then head to the ones that cost money. Make sure you check the discount information provided to save on admission fees to the various attractions. These discounts and bonuses often come with train or bus passes.

How to use the maps

Some Japanese cities and towns can be a nightmare to visit without a simple map, especially as most don't use street names. Detailed instructions for getting to places, and simple maps when appropriate, are provided so you won't spend time and money getting lost. Plus, you'll never need to get an expensive taxi. Use landmarks on the maps to help you get there as well, as Japanese streets can be difficult to navigate, even for those who have lived here many years.

Map Legend

- ⬆ Convenience store
- 🛒 Cheap supermarket
- ¥100 100 yen store
- ⊕ Pharmacy
- ? Tourist information
- 🚶 Recommended walking route
- ● Budget accommodation
- ⊤ Post office

Convenience stores are everywhere in Japan and have takeout meals from around 300 yen ($3). Finding a cheap supermarket can be a time-consuming hassle for budget travelers, so we have included cheap supermarkets in the guides. Prices are often slashed in the evenings to get rid of stock, so be sure to check them out for some ultra-cheap sushi!

100 yen stores (around $1) are even better for budget travelers. You can buy almost everything here, from drinks, to microwavable food, to gifts and clothing accessories. Japanese pharmacies and drug stores often have even cheaper prices for drinks and snacks as well.

Volunteer guides and tours

For those that want a more in-depth experience when visiting somewhere like a shrine or temple, using one of the vast number of free volunteer guide services is advised. For Tokyo, Kyoto and Osaka, these are listed in the introduction pages, while for other places recommended groups are listed individually in that location's chapter.

Budget food

Eating out cheaply

There are a host of cheap Japanese restaurant chains all over Japan, or focused on a particular region. These have been included on the easy-to-use maps, as well as in the Budget Food sections. As mentioned, cheap supermarkets and convenience stores are also included, to further help you keep your wallet happy!

Drinking on a budget

It is perfectly legal to drink outside in Japan, so budget travelers should get their alcohol fix at a convenience store or supermarket. You can then drink in parks, on the street or relax outside a train station and do a bit of people watching. If you want to check out the bars, get a few drinks in before to save money.

Water bottle refill spots

Most of the budget restaurants have water jugs to refill your bottle, and we have also included some other spots to refill, such as in parks. Buying a large bottled drink in a 100 yen shop, then using it for the rest of your trip is a great way to save on money. Also note that tap water is drinkable in Japan.

Types of accommodation

While we recommend hostels and hotels based on our own experiences and readers' feedback, always compare prices online. Recommended sites are Booking.com (usually free to cancel bookings) and Agoda (good choice in Asia) and of course Airbnb. For the budget traveler, the number of unacceptable rooms is almost zero, as quality and good customer service is so important in Japanese culture. Just make sure you are near a train stop or an easy-to-access bus stop so that you don't waste money and time finding your place. Also consider couch surfing (https://www.couchsurfing.com/) if you are really low on money.

Hostels and guesthouses

Japan has the best hostels and guesthouses in the world. Prices are reasonable, rooms are kept clean, beds linens are properly washed and

8

customer service is excellent. Sharing restrooms and showers is how people usually travel in Japan, so do what the locals do and save some cash on room fees.

Internet cafes

Net cafes are an even cheaper option, with prices often as low as 1000 yen. Stay in a small booth or even an open seat and chill out on the computer, or use the all-you-can-drink facilities. They can be tricky to find and confusing to use for people that don't speak Japanese, so they have been included in maps or detailed descriptions have been included in this guide, plus English translations of the sleeping options. Reservations are not possible online.

Love hotels

Love hotels are a great way to stay the night in any large city in Japan, if you are with that special someone. Each hotel usually has its own theme, so the best advice is to go to one of the areas we have listed, have a walk around, then settle on the hotel that looks best for you. Rates vary, so compare prices as you walk around, but they usually start from 6000 yen a night.

While it is usually the case that love hotel rooms have not been bookable, times are changing and websites such as Booking.com are starting to add them. It's still a fraction of what is available by just walking around though, so it's recommended not to book unless you are particularly nervous about going to one for the first time.

How to do a walk-in reservation at a love hotel

1) Love hotels usually have the rather Japanglish 'Rest' and 'Stay' written outside. Rest (レスト/休憩) means a stay of only a few hours, while Stay (宿泊) means to stay the night.
2) Once you are inside, there is usually an easy-to-understand picture display of rooms available. Select your room, then go and get your key. If only Japanese is written, 空室 means the room is available, 完全/満室 mean it is not.
3) You usually pay when you leave, but occasionally when you collect your key.

Capsule hotels

Capsule hotels, where guests sleep in small pods, are becoming increasingly popular with budget conscious travelers. We have included the best ones in the guides, and put them on maps for the relevant places. Many are now bookable online.

Staying in a capsule hotel will probably be one of the most interesting experiences you can have in Japan. Usually costing from 2000 to 3500 yen, depending on spa facilities and location, they offer a great way to stay the night in the city center. Most customers are usually businessmen who have missed their last train, so some are men only. But these days many offer women-only floors, so there's no need to worry about privacy. Note that most capsule hotels are usually just for the night, and will not allow you to keep your luggage there during the day. Check the rules if booking online. If you want to stay in a capsule hotel for more than one night, you can put your bags in lockers at a nearby station.

Overnight spas

Some hot springs or spas allow people to spend a little extra to stay the night. Guests usually sleep in lazyboy chairs or on tatami mats, with pillows and blankets provided. Great way to save on room costs, plus people are usually so sleepy after a long dip in the hot spring baths, that it doesn't matter if the sleeping arrangements are rather basic.

Campsites and mountain huts

For the countryside, bringing a tent or staying in mountain huts is an excellent way to stay a night on the cheap. Mountain huts are on hiking routes, so quite easy to find. Information has been included for campsites, as these can be tricky to find if you can't read Japanese. Always download the Google Maps data for the area, in case you get lost.

Free wifi locations

There are so many companies trying to sell expensive wireless adapters that connect to the phone networks. While this used to be essential when wifi was crappy here, wifi access has come leaps and bounds in the last few years. If you download and use the official Japan Connected-Free Wifi app, you can see all the free hotspots nearby, even if you are offline. Almost all the main tourist spots have free wifi these days, but this book contains extra information if it's especially tricky to find or use in the area.

Getting around

Trains and buses come regularly unless otherwise noted. There is usually no need to worry about checking the schedule in Japan, unless you are taking a limited express train. If it's possible, and interesting, to walk somewhere to save on train fares, walking route information has been included in the 'Walk and save!' sections and/or on the maps. Highway buses are also listed, as they usually sell tickets for far less than Shinkansen ones, and are highly recommended for budget travelers. Jorudan.com and Hyperdia are good websites for train travel, while Willer Express, Japan Bus Lines and Japan Bus Online are best for highway buses.

Travel costs

One of the reasons for making this book was to show that Japan isn't as expensive as people often say. With the help of this guide and Japan's efficient and convenient trains and shops, the country can be a perfect destination for budget travelers. Remember that with all the great transportation systems here, more can be done in one day than anywhere else.

Exchange rates
These are the rates as of June 2017. Check www.XE.com for the latest rates. 1 US Dollar = 111 yen • 1 Euro = 124 yen • 1 British Pound = 142 yen • 1 Canadian Dollar = 84 yen • 1 Australian Dollar = 84 yen

Average daily costs for budget travelers
Single Traveler: 6000-8000 yen, Two travelers: 5000-6000 yen per person, Multiple travelers: 4000-5000 yen per person

Usual prices
Dorm bed: 2000-3000 yen • Budget eat-in meal: 400-600 yen • Convenience store meal: 350-500 yen • Cup noodles: 100-190 yen • Bus ticket: 100-200 yen • Subway ticket: 140-240 yen

Electricity
East Japan (Tokyo, Yokohama) has an electrical current of 100v, 50Hz AC and the west (Osaka, Nagoya and Kyoto) uses 100v, 60Hz AC. Most devices such as phones and laptops will work fine, but appliances such as hair dryers and shavers can work slowly or may even get damaged without an adapter. Visitors from the UK and Europe will probably need to get an adapter, but those from North America may sometimes be fine as the shapes of the pins are identical. You can buy a cheap adapter at a duty-free shop in an airport or in any large electronics store.

Visas
Japan allows visa free travel from most countries for tourists, but make sure you check with the Japanese embassy where you live. Working holiday visas are also available for several nationalities.

Money
Japan is still very much a cash-based society. Most restaurants will not accept credit cards, but an increasing number accept IC cards, such as the Suica card used for train rides in Tokyo. Before heading off into the countryside, be sure to get enough cash from a convenience store in the city, otherwise you may be left without any money to buy food or get back

home! Also note that there is no tipping culture in Japan, which is good for budget travelers.

Coin lockers (コインロッカー)

Lockers are a great way to save money in Japan, or give more flexibility to budget travelers. Almost all stations in this guide have them. Stations are usually close to the tourist action. If you arrive somewhere early, it may be cheaper and more time efficient to put your luggage in a locker and check out the sights before checking in at your accommodation. Lockers are also useful if staying in accommodation, such as net cafes, that don't have private, secure areas to store your luggage.

Apps to download before you go

- Skyscanner and Kiwi.com for comparing cheap airplane tickets.
- Google Translate, then download the Japanese language pack in the app for offline use. Also translates text only using your phone camera.
- Japan Connected-Free Wifi, to find free wifi spots nationwide.
- Booking.com to quickly cancel or amend bookings. Airbnb is also worth downloading.
- Google Maps and Maps.me, plus in the apps download the areas you will be visiting for offline use.
- Navitime is also good for planning routes across Japan.
- XE Currency for comparing prices to back home.
- Splittr is a good app if traveling with friends. It allows you to add up and see who owes what to who.
- The Time Out apps have the latest listings for live events, new exhibitions and local festivals.

When to go to Japan

While for some countries the season that you go makes a huge difference in your travel plans, there is always a lot to do whatever time you decide to come to Japan. So if you see a great airplane ticket price in winter, go for it!

Spring (March to May)

Spring is the most popular time to come to Japan, so prices do increase a bit. It's cherry blossom season in Japan, and you will see beautiful pink and white trees everywhere. Before booking your hotels, make sure you check the cherry blossom blooming times online.

Summer (June to August)

Summer can get really hot and humid in Japan! Tokyo and Kyoto can get extremely hot, but there are countless free festivals to enjoy in the summer.

Autumn (September to November)

Autumn is also a great time to come because of the autumn leaves. Temperatures are much more comfortable across the whole country, but bring a jumper for the evening. Or head to budget clothing retailer Uniqlo to buy a tax-free one.

Winter (December to February)

The Christmas illuminations in Japan are some of the best in the world, and the main tourist attractions will be far less crowded than in other seasons. Many sites are closed for the New Year holidays and bus times can be less frequent, so be sure to check the closing days for the places you want to visit beforehand.

Peak seasons to avoid

As Japanese people usually all have their holidays at the same time, there are some dates when prices can skyrocket. It's still possible to find bargains, but such places can get quickly booked up. Try to avoid Golden Week (April 29th to May 5th), Obon holidays (around August 13th to 16th) and around the New Year holidays.

National passes and itineraries

There are three main national passes, each with their own pluses and minuses. In addition to these, there are many regional and city-wide passes. Budget travelers can choose to get a highway bus between these regional and city-wide passes, or do the whole thing on a national pass.

Japan Rail Pass

The pass most often used by first time travelers to Japan, but the increasing number of alternative passes is making it less popular for some budget travelers. It allows unlimited travel on all JR (national rail) trains all over Japan, including the Shinkansen and limited express trains. If you plan to ride on such trains, you can start to save money after just a few rides, so this pass offers excellent value for money if you want to quickly go to many different places over Japan. The pass can also be used for the JR Ferry to Miyajima and local JR buses (not highway buses). You must buy it at a travel agent in your home country or online before visiting Japan. For those with tourist visas only. *7 days: Adults 29110 yen, children 14550 yen. 14 days: Adults 46390 yen, children 23190 yen. 21 days: Adults 59350 yen, children 29670 yen*

Sample itinerary: The Japan Rail Pass for first timers to Japan
This is the most convenient way to see the highlights of Japan in one to two weeks. It could be started in Tokyo or Osaka, depending on where your

flight is arriving. You could then spend some time before and after the pass in these cities.

On the first day of using your pass, get on the Shinkansen from Tokyo to Kyoto. Spend a day or two there visiting the World Heritage shrines and temples, possibly in conjunction with the Kyoto City Bus One-Day Pass. Next head to Osaka to see what Japan's western capital is like, with its bustling downtown and friendly, outgoing people. On the next day visit Himeji, via Kobe if you want to see some foreign influenced culture and architecture, to see the newly-rebuilt Himeji castle, Japan's best. Next, continue further down west to visit Hiroshima, to learn about it's sad but important history, and Miyajima island to see the iconic Japanese torii gate floating on the see. When you are done, head back to Osaka or Tokyo on an evening Shinkansen. If you have time, try to include Okayama on the way back, to visit Japan's most stunning garden.

Japan Bus Pass

Willer Express covers all the main cities in this book, so the Willer Japan Bus Pass is a great option. It's the cheapest way to travel, especially if you want to save on hostel beds by using overnight buses. It cannot be used for local buses or short bus rides, so you will need to buy individual tickets or local transportation passes in the locations you visit. In other words, this pass is good for traveling long distances, but is not as flexible as a train pass. Get at the Willer Express website (http://willerexpress.com/en/) and check individual ticket prices to see if the pass is worth it for your trip plan. *All Routes MON to THU Pass: 3 Days 10000 yen, 5 Days 12500 yen, 7 Days 15,000 yen. All Routes ALL Day Pass (for use anytime of the week): 3 Days 12500 yen, 5 Days 15000 yen.*

Seishun 18

For real hardcore budget travelers. The Seishun 18 offers the best value for train travel in Japan. It does not allow the use of Shinkansen or limited express trains, so go for this pass if you don't mind longer journey times. It could also be a good choice if you don't want to stray too far from a particular hub, like Osaka or Tokyo, and want to visit places nearby. It provides five days of unlimited travel anywhere in Japan on JR trains (the national network), which do not need to be on consecutive days. Note that there are limited use periods, usually late July to early September and early December to early January. Buy it at any JR station. *11,850 yen •* http://www.jreast.co.jp/e/pass/seishun18.html

Tax-free shopping

Japan has a sales tax of 8%, going up to 10% in the future, but those with a tourist visa are eligible for tax-free shopping. If you love shopping and want to get some bargains, there has never been a better time to visit Japan. With a great exchange rate for most travelers and tax-free shopping, you'll be shopping till you drop!

What is most impressive about the latest tax-free shopping rules is that, while the main department stores and malls also offer it, almost all shops in tourist or cosmopolitan areas are offering tax-free shopping to tourists and actively promoting this. From cosmetics shops, to souvenir shops, to clothes shops such as Uniqlo, almost all are proudly displaying their tax-free signs. Almost 30,000 stores in Japan now offer tax-free shopping to tourists. All visitors need to do is head to their desired shops, follow the rules below and they can save loads of money.

How to do tax-free shopping in Japan

Unlike other countries, the tax-free system is usually in-store. Shops prominently tell you with bright signage if they are tax-free, so you are spoilt for choice in any city or tourist spot. Just show your passport and the tax will be taken off when you purchase. Some naughty shops levy a charge to get tax-free, so avoid these if it's mentioned.

Consumables (foods, drinks, medicines, cosmetics...)
Must be purchased at the same store on the same day, and the total spending must be more than 5000 yen, but no greater than 500,000 yen. Items must be taken out of Japan within 30 days of purchase.

Non-consumables (electric appliances, clothing, accessories...)
Must be purchased at the same store on the same day, and the total spending must be more than 5000 yen. Items must be taken out of Japan within six months of purchase.

At the airport
Be sure to keep the receipt you get when you buy your tax-free items. As you go through customs after checking in for your flight, there will be a counter (and often someone calling out "tax-free!!!") where you have to show this. Have the items ready to show, just in case they ask, as you may be asked to pay tax for a consumable item if you have already consumed it in Japan and cannot show it at the airport.

Top spots for tax-free shopping
For high end shopping, Ginza (銀座) in Tokyo has always been a great place to buy designer clothes, bags and watches. Also, an increasing number of lower end brands such as clothes megastore Uniqlo and electronic stores

have opened large stores in Ginza, so the area seems to be adapting a little to cater to a more budget-conscious clientele.

Other hot spots in Tokyo for tax-free shopping are Shinjuku, Shibuya and Akihabara. They all have the major electronic stores, department stores, cosmetic shops and travel stores for travelers to load up on tax-free goods. Outside of Tokyo, Namba in Osaka has a similar number of large shops to choose from, and Den Den Electric Town is the place to go for electronics.

Free festivals

Making sure you see one or two festivals, called matsuri in Japanese, is a good way to save money. Most are based on city streets or in temples, so entry is free and there are lots of stalls selling cheap snacks and more.

January
6th Dezome-shiki, Tokyo: Firemen show off their machines and do various stunts.
Fourth Saturday Wakakusa Yamayaki, Nara: Large grass burning ceremony on Mount Wakakusayama.
Sunday closest to 15th Toshiya, Sanjusangen-do Temple, Kyoto: Japanese archery contest.

February
3rd Setsubun Mantoro, Nara: More than 3,000 lanterns are lit up in Kasuga Taisha Shrine.
Third Saturday Saidai-ji Eyo Hadaka Matsuri, Okayama: About 10,000 almost naked men running through the streets, competing for good luck charms!

March
1st-14th Omizutori, Nara: In these ceremonies, Buddhist monks carry large flaming torches around Nigatsu-do Hall and then wave them over the side, raining embers down on the surrounding crowds below.

April
Second Sunday - Third Sunday Kamakura Festival, Kamakura: Ritual dance performances based on the samurai of medieval Japan.

May
The Saturday and Sunday closest to May 15th Kanda Matsuri, Tokyo: One of Tokyo's top three festivals. We go every year.
15th Aoi Matsuri, Kyoto: In this 1000-year-old event, participants wear ancient costumes and parade through downtown Kyoto.
18th Shunki Reitaisai, Nikko: Grand procession of 1,000 'samurai warriors' though the town.
Third Sunday and preceding Friday and Saturday Asakusa Sanja Matsuri, Asakusa, Tokyo: Amazing portable shrines are paraded throughout the town. Mind-blowing stuff.

Closest weekend to May 28th Hanazono Shrine Grand Festival, Shinjuku, Tokyo: Featuring ceremonial rites and dances, plus some cheap food stalls. On the Sunday, a huge 1.5 ton portable shrine (mikoshi) is taken on a tour of the surrounding neighborhoods.

June
14th Otaue Rice Planting Festival, Osaka: In Sumiyoshi Taisha Shrine, traditional dancing and songs are used to pray for a good harvest.
mid-June Sanno Matsuri, Tokyo: Another big festival in Tokyo, with a splendid procession of miniature shrines.

July
1st-31st Gion Matsuri, Kyoto: Huge golden floats parade through the main streets of Kyoto in this must-see event.
24th + 25th Tenjin Matsuri Festival, Osaka: Various events, such as 300-plus people dressed in imperial-court style clothing marching with portable shrines and one of the world's grandest boat processions.
Last Saturday Sumida River Fireworks, Tokyo: Tokyo's biggest and best fireworks display.

August
16th Daimonji Gozan Okuribi, Kyoto: Stunning bonfire event, as five of Kyoto's mountains are set on fire in motifs of Chinese characters.
Late August Awa-odori, Koenji, Tokyo: Awa-odori consists of nearly 200 Japanese dance groups showing off some spectacular traditional dances and music from across the country.
Last weekend Omotesando Genki Festival, Harajuku: Food festival which features the traditional yosakoi dance. It's one of the largest festivals in Tokyo and has more than 5000 energetic dancers from 100 plus groups performing.

September
14-16th Reitaisai, Kamakura: Horseback archery display and contest. Sure to make some awesome videos to put on Facebook.

October
22nd Jidai Matsuri, Kyoto: Traditional costume procession at Heian Jingu Shrine.
Sundays and national holidays Shika-no-Tsunokiri, Nara: This yearly ritual sees the local deer having their antlers sawn off, but the naughty ones can sure make it a difficult task for the skilled handlers. Near Kasuga Taisha Shrine.

November
3rd Hakone Daimyo Gyoretsu, Hakone: Around 200 people in samurai warrior and Japanese princess costumes parades around the hot spring town.

December
15th-18th Kasuga Wakamiya On-Matsuri, Nara: One of Nara's biggest festivals, full of traditional rituals, dances, music and a huge fireworks display.
Christmas and New Year lights Japan has some amazing illuminations, in particular at Terrace City, Shinjuku.

Cherry blossom viewing (花見)

Cherry blossoms in Inokashira Park, Kichijoji, Tokyo

Great for budget travelers, cherry blossoms are free to see all over Japan. From local gardens to shopping streets, you will never be more than a few minutes away from a sakura (cherry blossom) tree. They provide a perfect spot for a cheap meal or drink, as the tradition is to grab some cheap grub and beers from the local shops and enjoy them under the pink and white trees. Prices may be higher for some accommodations, but definitely not too much to deter a price conscious traveler. Surely one of the best times to visit Japan!

When to see cherry blossoms

There is a short window in which to see the cherry blossoms, so this can make it somewhat tricky for budget travelers. Train passes can really come in handy here, as if the weather changes before you visit and the conditions aren't quite right in the place you booked a hostel, you can quickly head somewhere better. For latest times check the official Japan national tourism site (http://www.jnto.go.jp/sakura/eng/index.php), but here are the averages from the last 10 years:
- Tokyo: First bloom 22nd March, full bloom 30th March
- Kyoto: First bloom 24th March, full bloom 3rd April
- Osaka: First bloom 25th March, full bloom 3rd April
- Hiroshima: First bloom 24th March, full bloom 2nd April

Best spots for cherry blossoms

There are great cherry blossom spots in every village, town and city in Japan, but here are our favorites:

Ueno Park

The biggest park in Tokyo for cherry blossoms, and it's all free. Can get super busy, but all the small stalls selling cheap food is a real plus.

Sumida Park

Along Sumida river in Asakusa, Tokyo. A fun, party atmosphere fills the park, which has a varied selection of cherry blossom trees.

Meguro River

A short walk from Meguro, the main action is around Naka-Meguro. This long, winding river is the coolest place to see the cherry blossoms, as it's lined with hip cafes and clothing shops. Come in the night with a beer or two.

Hachiman Shrine

See the big Buddha hanging out with all the cherry blossom trees in Kamakura. The grand, wide road leading up to the shrine is lined with cherry blossoms.

Yasaka Shrine

Head here first if on the lookout for cherry blossom trees in Kyoto. In the Gion area, this shrine is surrounded by large pink leaved trees. Nearby Maruyama Park is also worth visiting.

Philosopher's Walk

The Philosopher's Walk is another hotspot in Kyoto. There are cherry blossoms all along the way, plus a few attractions, such as small shrines surrounded by blossoming trees, to mix things up along the way.

Nara Park

Forget the cute deer, grab some low-cost food from the convenience store and head to this huge park in Nara. Usually lots of space to sit down, but no guarantees!

Himeji Castle

Himeji Castle is breath-taking during the cherry blossom season. The parks outside the castle are free, but it's worth paying the entrance fee to see this World Heritage site during such a breathtaking time of the year.

Japanese for budget travelers

The Japanese have a bad reputation for speaking English, but if you know some key phrases, this is not usually a problem. In all tourist spots or metropolitan areas, you are never too far from someone who speaks a bit of English. If you have trouble with the pronunciation, point at the Japanese text below. For individual words use Google Translate. If you are lost, show someone the Japanese in this book for the place you want to visit, as this will make it much easier for them to help you. Japanese people love to help, but can become very intimidated if they don't understand a foreigner.

Essential phrases

Do you speak English? - Eigo o hanasemas ka? / 英語を話せますか？
Hello! - Konnichiwa! / こんにちは！
Yes - Hai / はい
No - Iie / いえ
Thank you - Arigatou / ありがとう
Sorry - Sumimasen / すみません
I don't understand - Wakarimasen / わかりません
Please write down (e.g. number, price) - Kaite kudasai / かいてください
Where is the _? - _ wa doko des ka? / _はどこですか？

Insert the following above to ask for directions:
Toilet = Toire / トイレ • Train station = Eki / えき • Subway station = Chikatetsu / ちかてつ

Shopping

How much is this? - Ikura des ka? / いくらですか？
Do you have _? - _ arimas ka? / _ありかすか？

Getting food and drink

Do you have an English menu? - Eigo no menyu wa arimas ka? / 英語のメニューはありかすか？
I'd like _ please - _ o kudasai / _をください
That please - Kore o kudasau / これをください (point at the item)
Water please (save on drinks) - Omizu o kudasai / お水をください
Refill please! (use if free refills available) - Okawari! / おかわり！
Takeout please - Teiku-auto de / テイクアウトで
Eat-in please - Eeto-in de / イートインで
Is there a cover or table charge? - Charji arimas ka? / チャージありますか？

Traveling around

Please tell me when we get to _. (good for buses/trains with no English signs) - _ ni tsuku toki ni oshiete kudasai / _に着くときに教えてください

Tokyo

Kaminarimon, Asakusa

Tokyo is the capital city of Japan and one of the most densely-populated cities in the world. More than 13 million people live in the center, while the greater Tokyo metropolis houses over 35 million. Tokyo is very much a 'city of cities', with each one having its own distinct feel and attractions. We would therefore recommend heading to the highlights, and from these spots head off to other sites of interest. The fact that all these cities are connected by an excellent, and cheap, subway network means that budget travelers can do lots in one day.

A little bit of history

Tokyo is actually a relatively new capital. In 1590 the Shoguns, Japan's military dictators, moved from Kyoto to Edo, the old name for Tokyo. While the emperor stayed in Kyoto, the real power and money moved to the new city. In the early 17th century, Edo blossomed under Shogun Tokugawa Ieyasu and spread out around Edo Castle. The city still remained cut off from the rest of the world, though.

The Shogunate finally fell in 1867, bringing Emperor Meiji into power. He renamed the city Tokyo, meaning 'eastern capital', and opened up Japan's borders to the world. Foreign culture and technology, particularly from the west, flooded into the country via ports such as Yokohama. Japan really started to become important on the world scene.

In 1923, Tokyo was devastated by the Great Kanto Earthquake. More than 2 million people were left homeless and more than 100,000 perished. The city was further damaged by the bombing in World War Two, which destroyed much of the capital. Thankfully Tokyo experienced rapid growth after the war, and has become a real success story as the most vibrant, exciting and fascinating city in the world.

Highlights

1) Shinjuku
Tokyo's best cosmopolitan spot, Shinjuku is fall of budget superstores, great low-cost food and a high number of tax-free shops.

2) Harajuku
Tokyo's best spot for all things kawaii (cute). Cheap clothes, accessories and some amazing trendsetting fashion from the locals.

3) Mount Takao
The essential hiking day trip from Tokyo. Super cheap to access, easy to navigate and all you can drink beer at the top!

4) Shimo-Kitazawa
A maze of narrow streets, that look completely unchanged from the 50's or 60's. No ugly skyscrapers here.

5) Shibuya
Featuring Tokyo's most photographed area, the Shibuya Pedestrian Scramble, this hyperactive area has lots of people watching and window shopping opportunities for budget travelers.

6) Edo-Tokyo Museum
Offers the most comprehensive information on Tokyo's history, architecture and culture. The low price more than pays for itself.

7) Tokyo Metropolitan Observation Decks
Skip the pricey SkyTree and head to this free observation deck for a spectacular view over the city.

Volunteer guides

There are several organizations offering free guide services in Tokyo, so we will just list the best ones. For more visit the official list at
http://www.jnto.go.jp/eng/arrange/travel/guide/list_volunteerGuides.php

Tokyo International Student Guide - https://www.facebook.com/tsgg.for.tourists/
A bunch of friendly students from local universities and colleges who are
eager to show tourists around. They focus on top spots in Tokyo, but can
accommodate special requests.

Tokyo SGG Club - http://tokyosgg.jp/guide.html
More focused on the east side, such as the museum, parks and shrines
around Asakusa and Ueno. No reservation is required, you just need to show
up at one of their tourist information centers and tag along!

Tokyo Free Guide - http://www.tokyofreeguide.org/
Another well-known service in Tokyo. It's a free guide service with the aim
to encourage cultural exchanges between Japanese people and foreigners.
Services are available in multiple languages, such as English, French, Italian
and Spanish.

IC cards

The main IC card in Tokyo is the Suica card, available to buy at any ticket
machine from a JR station in Tokyo. Journey prices are a little cheaper when
using the card, so if you are in Tokyo for more than a few days then you can
save a little. They also reduce the chance of overpaying when transferring
between lines, which can be confusing. The Suica card also works on all the
subway lines and buses in Tokyo. *2000 yen (500 yen deposit, 1500 yen put on
card)*

How to get there and away

By air

There are two main airports for Tokyo, Narita Airport (NRT) and Haneda
Airport (HND). When choosing your flight, it doesn't really matter which one
you choose as there are cheap transportation options from both.

Narita Airport transportation

Access Narita and Keisei both offer 1000 yen buses into the city (1 hour, 100
yen off Keisei bus if pre-booked). Access Narita goes to/from Tokyo station
and Ginza, while Keisei also goes to Odaiba. These are the cheapest options
for budget travelers, but it's also possible to use the Keisei local and express
line trains to/from Nippori station in Tokyo (1 hour, 1240 yen).

Haneda Airport transportation

Haneda is much closer to downtown Tokyo, so it's usually cheaper and
easier to just use the Keikyu Line or **Monorail**. Take the Keikyu Line to
Shinagawa (11 mins, 410 yen) or the **Monorail** to Hamamatsucho (19 mins,
490 yen), then transfer from these hubs.

By train
If you are far from Tokyo and have the Japan Rail Pass, you should take the Shinkansen to Tokyo or Shinagawa station.

By bus
If you are traveling far from Tokyo, such as from Kyoto, Osaka or Hiroshima, and don't have a Japan Rail Pass then it's much, much cheaper to take the bus. Check prices at Japan Bus Lines, Willer Bus and JR Bus Kanto.

Discount transportation passes

There are three main passes for travel in central Tokyo that will be of most use to budget travelers. Note that in central Tokyo there are three main networks: Tokyo Metro (main subway network), Toei Subway (only four lines) and JR trains. These passes are a great way to save a bit of cash when doing a lot in one day, and also give extra flexibility to try somewhere new if you have a bit of free time. The pass you choose really depends on where you want to visit, so check the 'Recommended rail passes' for each place. The easiest way is to get the Tokyo Subway Ticket on the first day, then see how much you can get done on that.

At the time of writing, the one-day passes for the subway networks also come with a 'Chikatoku' discount booklet, which allows pass owners to get discounts or free bonus items at more than 400 locations in Tokyo. See http://chikatoku.enjoytokyo.jp/en/ for the full list.

Tokyo Subway Ticket 24h/48h/72h
New pass available only to foreign tourists, so you need to show a passport when purchasing. This awesome ticket allows use of both Toei Subway and Tokyo Metro. Available at Haneda or Narita Airport, or some Bic Camera or Laox Tax Free shops. See http://www.tokyometro.jp/en/ticket/value/travel/ for more locations. *24 hours: Adults 800 yen, children 400 yen. 48 hours: Adults 1200 yen, children 600 yen. 72 hours: Adults 1500 yen, children 750 yen*

Tokyo Metro 24-hour Ticket
If you have no need to also use the Toei Subway, then get this pass instead, and save a few hundred yen. This may require longer journey times to some destinations, but it's the cheapest way to get around the city. *Adults 600 yen, children 300 yen*

Tokyo Metropolitan District Pass (Tokunai Pass)
A good option if you are going to main transportation hubs like Akihabara, Shibuya, Tokyo or Shinjuku stations or want to venture a little into the suburbs, such as to Koenji or Ryogoku. This pass allows unlimited use of JR trains only, and includes all their trains in central Tokyo, plus a little distance

outside. Available at all JR stations in central Tokyo. *Adults 700 yen, children 370 yen*

Sample day itineraries

Cool Tokyo
First head to Harajuku to see what's trending in everything kawaii (cute fashion), before dropping into Shibuya to see Japan's top brands. After lunch, geek out in Akihabara and visit Asakusa for Tokyo's most popular temple. Then head to Koenji for a more down-to-earth vibe in the evening. Perfect with the Tokyo Metro 24-hour Ticket.

Tradition and history in Tokyo
Good with the Tokyo Subway Ticket, first go to Ryogoku to visit the free Sumo museum and then the Edo-Tokyo museum, to learn all about Tokyo's history. After lunch head to Ueno, to see the free temples in Ueno park and the traditional markets. If you have time, be sure to check out Hama Rikyu Garden and the nearby Imperial Palace gardens. In the early evening, continue to Ebisu to enjoy the Museum of Yebisu Beer.

The big, big city
Using the Tokyo Metropolitan District Pass, you can see lots of the most exciting, bustling areas, all in a day. Start in Shinjuku, where you can go up the observation tower to get a view over the city and see the huge Shinjuku Gyoen park. After lunch, proceed to Shibuya for some photo taking, especially of the super busy pedestrian crossing. Head east for the Imperial gardens and views of the classically designed Tokyo station. Finally head to Sugamo for some discount shopping and relax in the hot spring.

Grutto Pass (ぐるっとパス)

For most budget travelers wanting to check out a gallery or two, the latest listings on TimeOut Tokyo are worth checking out. Many of them are free. But for real gallery and museum junkies, the Grutto Pass should be considered. Unlike many countries, most museums in Japan charge entry fees, so costs can add up. The Grutto Pass provides free admission or discounts to 79 art galleries, museums, zoos and more in Tokyo. If you want to visit many museums and galleries in Tokyo, you will really start to save some money. Count up the cost and see how much you could save at the official website (http://www.rekibun.or.jp/grutto/english.html) before getting the pass. *2000 yen. Note that there is also a Tokyo Metro & Grutto Pass 2017 Pass, which also includes two days of subway travel for 2700 yen.*

Tokyo Budget Accommodation

Tokyo has a superb selection of budget accommodation, from female-only hostels to countless net cafes allowing overnight stays.

Hostels and Guest Houses

While these are the best ones we have stayed at in Tokyo, horror stories are almost nonexistent, so feel free to go for the cheapest one online!

Khaosan Hostels

This well-known guesthouse chain has a variety of cheap and clean guesthouses in central locations. They all have their own unique theme, so they are a bit nicer to stay at than a dull YHA hostel. *Dorms from 2200 yen, private rooms from 3400 yen* • http://khaosan-tokyo.com/en/

Tokyo Central Youth Hostel

A clean, reasonably priced hostel (especially if you are a Hostelling International Member) right bang in the center of Tokyo. Great for large groups. *Dorms from 3360 yen • Above Iidabashi station (JR and Metro lines)* • http://www.jyh.gr.jp/tcyh/e/top.html

Shrek Watta House

A nice guesthouse, we have stayed here several times. Has both western and Japanese style tatami mat rooms. Run by a nice old man, this place has a nice open kitchen with loads of free travel resources. *Private rooms from 2150 yen • Musashi-Seki station, near Shinjuku station •* http://www.shrek-watta-house.com/index.html

Anne Hostel Asakusabashi

Free breakfast is provided at this friendly hostel. Highly recommended by many travelers. *Dorms from 2800 yen, private rooms from 3400 yen • Near Ueno and Akihabara*

Tatami Guesthouse

A bit further away than most others, but we have stayed here and would highly recommend the place. It's very cheap, is in a quiet area and there are lots of people around to help you in your travels (one Japanese guy took us on a free tour of an animation museum!). *Private rooms from 2100 yen • Hibarigaoka station •* http://www.tatami-guesthouse.com/

GrapeHouse Koenji (female only)

This ladies only hostel has a great reputation and gets full up easily, so try to book as early as possible. Friendly staff can help you to get around. *Dorms from 3500 • Koenji station •* http://grapehouse.jp/en/

Love hotels (adults only)

Shinjuku

Kabukicho is a heartland for love hotels, so head to the northern area if you don't have a reservation and want to see what's available. The ones available to reserve online are often two or three times as expensive as just turning up, but try

Booking.com if you want that peace of mind. *'Rest' (2-4 hours) from 1500 yen, 'Stay' (overnight) from 6500 yen*

Shibuya Love Hotel Hill

Head to Love Hotel Hill (ラブホテル坂) for a bewildering range of love hotels. Take your time to compare prices and facilities available. No need to book in advance as there is so much choice here. *'Rest' (2-4 hours) from 1500 yen, 'Stay' (overnight) from 6500 yen*

Capsule hotels
Akihabara

Capsule Value Kanda (men only)

You will soon realize why they have a 91% rating. Really helpful staff, cheap bike rental and inexpensive rooms. *Capsules from 2400 yen • From Kanda station, take the south exit, walk down the track and take left turn at 2nd road under track •* http://capsuleinn.com/kanda/en/

First Cabin Akihabara

More upmarket than Capsule Value, with spacious capsules and hotel like facilities. *Capsule from 3700 yen • From Metro Hibiya exit 4, 1 min down 2nd road parallel to river*

Asakusa

Capsule Hotel Asakusa River Side

A very cheap capsule hotel with English support, right next to Asakusa station. *Capsules from 2000 yen • Opposite exit A5*

Shibuya

Capsule and Sauna Century Shibuya (Men only) (カプセルホテル渋谷)

Cheap capsule hotel right in the center of Shibuya. *Capsules from 3500 yen • West side of Shibuya station*

Shinjuku

Hatagoya (カプセルホテルはたごや)

Looks more like a new ryokan (Japanese hotel) from the outside, this new capsule hotel is modern, clean and has free soap and shampoo in the showers. *Capsules from 3200 yen •* http://hatago-ya.com/

nine hours Shinjuku-North (ナインアワーズ 北新宿)

This trustworthy capsule hotel chain has recently opened a new branch in Shinjuku. Great English-language support at the 24h front desk. *Capsules from 3000 yen •* https://ninehours.co.jp/

Overnight Spas (super sentos)

Oedo-Onsen Monogatari Hot Spring (大江戸温泉物語)

It's also possible to stay the night here in Odaiba's huge onsen, where you can sleep in the tatami rooms or in the lazyboy chairs. *2160 yen extra to stay overnight*

Internet cafes
Akihabara
You are really spoilt for choice here, so here are just a few safe bets.

Comcom (コムコム)
Good choice of free drinks, 100 yen snacks, plus free blanket and slippers for a good night's sleep. Showers 300 yen. *Night pack (ナイトパック) available from 5pm: 6 hours (6 時間ナイトパック) from 1230 yen, 9 hours (9 時間ナイトパック) from 1850 yen (show coupon pic at* http://www.iicomcom.com/coupon/ *for 200 yen off) • Head out of Electric Town exit, and head to Chuo Dori (main street). It's near the train bridge, on the left*

Ai Cafe Akiba Place (アイ・カフェ)
Huge choice of comics, drinks and ice cream. Also has free food! Rice bowls, toast and curry on the house. Note the cheapest prices are for cafeteria seats. *Night pack (ナイトパック) available from 6pm: 6 hours (6 時間ナイトパック) from 1060 yen, 9 hours (9 時間ナイトパック) from 1660 yen • Head up Chuo Dori and take first left after Don Quijote*

Shibuya
Head down Inokashira Dori, parallel to Center Gai for a good selection of net cafes:

Bagus (バグース)
Large choice of comics, clean showers and good selection of free drinks. *Night pack (ナイトパック) available from 9pm: 6 hours (6 時間ナイトパック) from 1150 yen. 9 hours (9 時間ナイトパック) from 1800 yen*

Manbo (マンボー)
Japan's largest chain. Free showers, comics and drinks. *Night pack (ナイトパック) available from 7pm: 6 hours (6 時間ナイトパック) from 1300 yen*

Media Cafe Popeye (メディアカフェポパイ)
Modern net cafe with free drinks, showers and printing services. *Night pack (ナイトパック) available from 6pm: 6 hours (6 時間ナイトパック) from 950 yen. 12 hours (12 時間ナイトパック) from 1380 yen*

Shinjuku

Manbo (マンボー)
This net cafe chain has several chains around the station, so if this branch is full, ask for the others. Free showers, comics and drinks. *Night pack (ナイトパック) available from 7pm: 6 hours (6 時間ナイトパック) from 1500 yen • Head down Yasukuni Dori, passing east side Yamada Denki LABI. Manbo is just after the Family Mart, on the right*

Bagus (バグース)
Similar to Manbo, but generally quieter and with not so bright lights, so it's easier to sleep. Also has a ladies-only section. *Night pack (ナイトパック) available from 7pm: 6 hours (6 時間ナイトパック) from 1150 yen. 9 hours (9 時間ナイトパック) from 1430 yen • Next block on from above Manbo*

Shinjuku (新宿)

Shinjuku Gyoen in autumn

A great place to start of your adventures in Japan, Shinjuku is the main business and entertainment district in Tokyo. While Shibuya is well and truly aimed at younger people, Shinjuku is a bit more sophisticated than its southern brother. It's therefore a great place to introduce yourself to that Japanese mix of old and new.

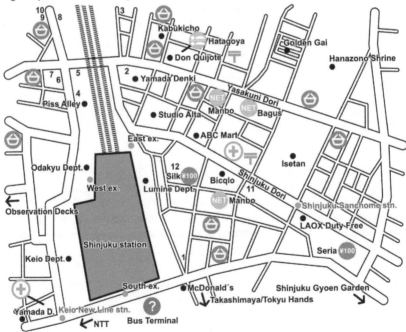

A little bit of history

While many people have an image of Tokyo being completely full of skyscrapers, this is in fact not the case, with the city having several pockets of skyscraper districts. In 1923, when the Great Kanto earthquake obliterated most of Tokyo, west Shinjuku was left relatively unscathed due to its seismically stable location. It therefore developed as a business district, full of grand skyscrapers. In the following years, most of Tokyo was destroyed by air raids in World War Two, but the pre-war form of Shinjuku was retained to ease reconstruction, with the exception of Kabukicho. There are still therefore plenty of interesting narrow streets to explore, and a short walk will get visitors away from all the commercial activity.

Things to do

Shinjuku Gyoen Garden (新宿御苑)

Usually a must see for any visitor to Tokyo, Shinjuku Gyoen National Garden is a large, feature-full park next to Shinjuku station. The garden was previously the mansion grounds of the Naito family, feudal lords in the Edo period. Every visitor makes a trip here when coming to Shinjuku, but as this garden is so large and varied it never seems overcrowded. In addition to the traditional Japanese garden and small pavilion, there are French and English inspired gardens, a small forest with Japanese cedar trees and a brand new, ultra-modern greenhouse. *Adults 200 yen, Children 50 yen • 9am-4pm • On Foot: From Shinjuku station, make your way to Bicqlo (ビックロ). Walk east (past Isetan Department Store), down Shinjuku Dori (street) until you get to Sekaido stationery shop (世界堂), then turn right and walk down for the entrance. By subway: Take the Metro Marunouchi Line from Shinjuku to Shinjuku-gyoen-mae (2 mins, 165 yen). By bus: Shinjuku Gyoen stop (WE Bus)*

Tokyo Metropolitan Observation Decks (東京都庁)

The free Tokyo Metropolitan Government Office offers great views of the city during daytime and evening, plus on clear days you can even see Mount Fuji. You can also buy your name in Japanese characters in the gift shop at the top. Save on the cost of the expensive SkyTree and visit here instead! *FREE • 9:30am-11pm (entry ends 30 minutes before closing) • On foot: Walk west for 10 minutes from Shinjuku station in the underground passageway to Tochomae station, then continue five minutes west. By subway: Take the Toei Oedo Line from Shinjuku station to Tochomae station (2 mins, 174 yen). By bus: Shinjuku Washington Hotel stop (WE Bus)*

Hanazono Shrine (花園神社)

Lovely respite from the chaos of Shinjuku, a cool place to chill out and have a bento or snack. Hanazono is a Shinto shrine founded in the 17th century and is considered to be one of the most important in Tokyo by locals, which explains why it's still there with all the huge concrete buildings around it. The shrine has become a favorite for local businessmen to pray for business success and prosperity. *FREE • 24h • On foot: Walk down Shinjuku Dori, take a left after Isetan Department Store and walk down (total 15 mins). By subway: Shinjuku-Sanchome exit E2. By bus: Shinjuku Oiwake stop (WE Bus)*

Kabukicho (歌舞伎町)

Tokyo's, and Japan's, most famous red light district. For budget travelers, it's a fascinating walk around, taking in all the bright lights, watching the nightclub and bar hosts and hostesses getting up to their business. It's generally recommended to stay away from bars and restaurants here, as prices are generally high and foreigners have been known to be overcharged. Just bring your camera after dark and take it all in. *Just outside Shinjuku station, take the east exit and walk towards Seibu Shinjuku station, right next to Kabukicho*

NTT InterCommunication Center (NTT インターコミュニケーション・センター)

Free media, art and communications gallery in Nishi-Shinjuku, the skyscraper district. NTT is Japan's main telephone provider, and this museum was started to commemorate the 100th anniversary of telephones in Japan. The museum has an excellent selection of innovative, fun and thought-provoking art and multimedia pieces, and shows off some amazing new artists. *FREE (extra for special exhibitions, which are FREE with Grutto Pass) • 11am-6pm • On foot: Near the Keio New Line station. Walk along the main road (Shinjuku dori) in the opposite direction of the bridge and Bus Terminal. By subway: From Shinjuku, take the Keio New Line to Hatsudai station (1 min, 124 yen). By bus: Shinjuku Washington Hotel stop (WE bus)*

Volunteer guides and tours

The tourist information center in the Tokyo Metropolitan Building (see above) can organize free volunteer tours in English.

Getting around

Once you are at Shinjuku station, everywhere is within walking distance if you don't mind walking for 5-15 minutes to get between tourist spots. The shops around the station are also close, taking only a few minutes between each one. There are two main streets, Shinjuku Dori to the south and Yasukuni Dori to the north.
Be warned! Shinjuku station is a complete maze and even for people that have worked there for years, it can be easy to get lost. Use the in-station signs to get to one of the above shops or tourist sites if you are completely lost, from where you can get your bearings.

Transportation passes and discounts

There is also a bus service called WE Bus (新宿 WE バス) that takes riders around the main spots listed above, from 7am-6pm (100 yen each ride, 300 yen for day pass). Tickets and passes available on the bus, with the most useful route being the Shinjuku Gyoen + Nishi-Shinjuku Route. Starting at the Shinjuku Bus Terminal near Shinjuku station, south exit is recommended, to avoid traipsing around the huge station looking for the right bus stop.

Budget food

Around the station (east side)

There are so many cheap restaurants around Shinjuku (usually with English menus), we would actually recommend strolling around this fascinating metropolis and seeing what takes your fancy. Here are some of the highlights if you are too hungry to walk around!

1) Senka Soba (千曲そば) - Various styles of simple soba and udon available, with simple traditional toppings such as tempura or egg. *Soba from 250 yen • 24h • From the south-east exit, take the wide stairs down and walk ahead, it's on the corner*

2) Yoshinoya (吉野家) - Gyudon eat-in and takeaway. *Meals from 330 yen • 24h • Next to Yamada Denki (LABI) on Yasukuni Dori*

3) Hidakaya Ramen (日高屋) - Tokyo's super cheap ramen chain. Fried rice and gyoza dumplings also available. *Ramen from 390 yen • 24h • Opposite Seibu-Shinjuku station, or next to Yamada Denki (LABI) on Yasukuni Dori*

Around the station (west side)

Hakone Soba Honjin (箱根そば本陣) - Classic train station soba, nice and simple. Other simple dishes like curry are also sometimes available. *Soba from 290 yen • 6:30am-11pm • Near ticket gates for Odakyu trains on west side of station*

4) Coco Ichiban Curry House (CoCo 壱番屋) - The true taste of Japanese curry, and officially the largest curry restaurant chain in the world. *Curry + rice from 500 yen • 24h • Just outside exit D3, from Shinjuku-Nishiguchi station on the Toei Oedo Line*

5) Matsuya (松屋) - Gyudon and burger eat-in and takeaway. *Gyudon bowls from 290 yen • 24h • Around the corner from the above Coco Ichiban*

6) Ootoya (大戸屋) - Various Japanese set meals. *Meals from 750 yen • 11am-midnight • Opposite from above Coco Ichiban restaurant*

7) Oedo Sushi (回転寿司 大江戸) - Reliable conveyor belt sushi joint. *Sushi plates from 140 yen • 11am-11pm • Next to the above Ootoya*

North-west of the station

Take exit D5 of Shinjuku-Nishiguchi station, or walk from Shinjuku station. The following are in the order you'll see them:

8) Mos Burger (モス) - Mid-range burger chain, for those that need a western food fix with some Japanese twists, like 'rice burgers'. *Burgers from 220 yen • 5am-2am*

9) Sukiya (すき家) - Curry and gyudon eat-in and takeaway. *Meals from 360 yen • 24h*

10) Burger King (バーガーキング) - Cheaper burgers than Mos Burger, and a few odd Japan-only burgers. Occasionally has all-you-can eat whopper deals! *Burgers from 150 yen • 7am-11pm*

Shinjuku Dori (Street)

There are not so many budget options heading east down Shinjuku Dori from Shinjuku station, but it's still a supremely cool street to check out.

11) Shakey's (シェーキーズ) - All-you-can-eat pizza restaurant, with Japanese and seasonal themed flavors. Expect to be surprised by this imaginative menu! *Lunch* *time: adults 1160 yen, teens 880 yen, under junior high school age 500 yen. Dinner time: 1650 yen, 1000 yen, 500 yen • 11am-10:15pm • On right side, just before Isetan Department Store*

12) Sweets Paradise (スイーツパラダイス) - Stuff yourself at this all-you-can-eat sweets and cakes buffet. *Adults 1530 yen, children 860 yen • Look for the old Bic Camera building on your right as you exit from Shinjuku station, east exit. Sweets Paradise is just to the right, away from Shinjuku Dori •* http://www.sweets-paradise.jp/guide/index_english.html

Nightlife

Piss Alley / Omoide Yokocho (思い出横丁)

Super cramped bar and counter restaurant area, this place requires a photo or two for being such an authentic Japanese night out spot. Prices have been increased to catch out tourists at some bars, so be careful if you want to eat or drink here. *Head out of Shinjuku west exit and then down to the right, or go out of exit D3 near Coco Ichiban restaurant. Bar area is around and behind here •* http://www.shinjuku-omoide.com/english/

Golden Gai (新宿ゴールデン街)

A maze of more than 100 tiny bars to explore. Staff are often chatty and will offer great travel advice. Many of the bars have a cover charge, so look at the board outside or ask inside. Still really worth a walk around if you are not going in though, just to see how crammed in all the bars are. *Head east down Yasukuni Dori until you get to Mister Donut on the left after five to 10 minutes. Walk down the spiraling path*

Water bottle refill spots

The Tokyo Metropolitan Government Office and Shinjuku Gyoen have water fountains, plus Isetan Department store has a water cup machine on the stairs up from the 1st floor.

Shopping

East side

Yamada Denki LABI

Modern electronics megastore, with tax-free and electronics for use abroad. There is also a quieter branch on the west side. *10am-11:30 pm • From Shinjuku station, east exit, head north along the tracks, it's on the right on Yasukuni Dori*

Don Quijote (ドン・キホーテ)

Chaotic megastore full of any item you could imagine, from cheap souvenirs to fancy dress costumes to travel goods. This store is maybe the premier 'what the hell is going on?' Don Quijote experience. Great prices and tax-free options available. *24h • Opposite Yamada Denki LABI on Yasukuni Dori*

Bicqlo (ビックロ)

Bic Camera (huge electronics store with tax-free shopping) + Uniqlo (huge budget clothes store with tax-free shopping) = a budget traveler heaven! Also has GU,

Uniqlo's new budget shop brand. *10am-10pm • East down Shinjuku Dori, not far from station*

LAOX Duty Free (ラオックス)
Mainly aimed at Chinese and Korean tourists looking to buy tax-free bags, jewelry and perfume. Worth having a quick look inside to see if a bargain can be had. *9am-9pm • Across the road from Isetan*

Tokyu Hands (東急ハンズ)
Tokyu Hands has everything from stationery to DIY goods to funny souvenirs and drinks. A bit more upmarket than Don Quijote, but prices can still be reasonable if doing tax-free shopping and looking out for special offers. *10am-9pm • Connected to Takashimaya department store*

ABC Mart (ABC マート)
Cheap shoe shop chain, with everything from sneakers to business shoes. *11am-9pm • Down Shinjuku Dori, just before Bicqlo*

Free sample hotspots
Isetan Department Store on Shinjuku Dori and Takashimaya have massive food courts in their basement floors. While the average item is quite pricey, there are plenty of free samples to be had, and it's also a fascinating window shopping experience. Just keep an eye out and don't make it look too obvious if you're not going to buy anything!

100 yen shops
Silk (シルク) - Near Yodobashi Camera on the east side. *10am-11pm*
Seria (セリア) - Inside Marui Annex on Shinjuku Dori. *11am-9pm*

Pharmacy (ドラッグストア)
Matsumoto Kiyoshi (マツモトキヨシ) has a shop opposite Bicuro (9am-10:30pm), while on the west side the best is Daikoku Drug (ダイコクドラッグ), near Yamada Denki (8am-midnight).

How to get there and away

Shinjuku is on the circular Yamanote Line, Toei Oedo Line, Metro Marunouchi Line or Metro Shinjuku Line. From Tokyo station, take the Chuo Line to Shinjuku station (14 mins, 190 yen). From Shibuya station, take the Saikyo Line to Shinjuku station (6 mins, 150 yen). *Recommended rail passes: Tokyo Subway Ticket, Tokyo Metro 24-hour Ticket, Tokyo Metropolitan District Pass*

Tourist information (観光案内所)

A large tourist information center is found on the 1st floor of the Tokyo Metropolitan Building. It has excellent, free maps for hiking (9:30am-6:30pm). Shinjuku Bus Terminal also has one (6:30am-11pm).

Shibuya (渋谷)

One of Tokyo's most lively and colorful neighborhoods, Shibuya is most famous as a youth fashion hotspot and the busiest road crossing you will ever see. Originally the site of a castle belonging to the Shibuya clan, since the introduction of the Yamanote Line it has become one of the main clubbing, shopping and entertainment areas in Tokyo.

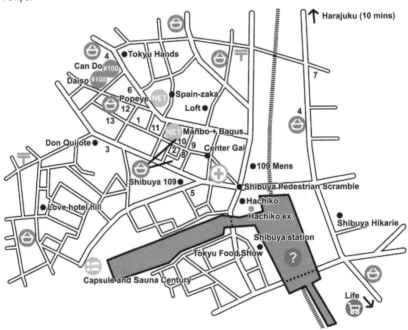

The station is a real maze, so use the locations on the map (e.g. Hachiko or Shibuya Hikarie) with the boards inside the station that direct visitors to the corresponding exits.

Things to do

Free activities near station

Shibuya pedestrian scramble (スクランブル交差点)
Every few minutes thousands of people walk over the world's most famous road crossing. Make sure you bring a camera! Best spot is to head to the second floor of Starbucks. *Hachiko exit*

Hachiko statue (ハチ公)
The famous statue and meeting point in Shibuya. After his owner died, a dog called Hachiko came to the station every day to meet his owner. The dog became famous and this statue was made in dedication to him. A cute cat has also made the statue its home, so be sure to take a photo of Shibuya's most iconic spot. *Hachiko exit*

Love hotel hill (ラブホテル坂)
Shibuya is an expensive place to live, so many people still live with their family. Many therefore head over to this prized love hotel area for a bit of privacy with their partner. This area is full of these hotels offering rooms for very cheap prices. Even if you are not staying, it's definitely worth a walk around to see all the cheesy architecture and bright lights. *All night! • Take a left after Don Quijote and walk up*

Free sample heavens

Tokyu Food Show (東急フードショー)
A treasure chest of Japanese food, plus international stalls to spice things up. With countless stalls, you can spend lots of time just wandering around, trying out free samples as you go. *10am-9pm • Basement of Tokyu Department Store, west side of station*

Shibuya Hikarie (渋谷ヒカリエ)
A new department store with modern shops, restaurants and a nice food area downstairs. Has even more stalls handing out free samples than Tokyu Food Show, so try lots and see what you like. *10am-9pm • Exit 15 / east exit*

Center Gai (渋谷センター街)
Shibuya's main shopping street, also known as Basketball Street. Center Gai is full of game arcades, fast food restaurants, fashion boutiques and bars. The food options are excellent and the area comes to life in the evening, with plenty of raucous businessmen and teenagers. *Across the Shibuya pedestrian scramble*

Shopping around Shibuya station

Shibuya 109
Worth a walk around to see what is hot and what is not in the world of youth fashion in Japan. 109 is the place to be for upcoming brands, and regarded as a stamp of

quality for them. Staff are very friendly and will help you out if you don't know what things are! *10am-9pm • Exit 3A*

Tokyu Hands (東急ハンズ)

Full of crazy, strange Japanese goods for you to laugh at and enjoy. Back scratchers, weird massage chairs, crazy robot toys and some unimaginable goods. Great for souvenirs and any novelties you want to take home. *10am-9pm • 5 minutes down Inokashira Dori*

Don Quijote (ドン・キホーテ)

Cheaper prices than Tokyu Hands, this megastore has everything from second-hand jewelry to clothes, to cheap snacks. They also have takeout sushi and other items for lunch. *10am-4:30am • Exit 3A, then down the road to left*

100 yen shops

Can Do (キャンドゥイ) - Opposite Tokyu Hands. *10am-10pm*
Daiso (ダイソー) - Another great 100 yen shop nearby. *10am-9pm*

Pharmacy (ドラッグストア)

Matsumoto Kiyoshi (薬 マツモトキヨシ) is on the way to 109 (24h).

Budget food

Budget chain restaurants on map

1) Tenka Ippin (天下一品) - ramen. *Ramen from 700 yen • 11am-3am*
2) Matsuya (松屋) - rice bowls and curry. *Gyudon bowls from 290 yen • 24h*
3) Ootoya (大戸屋) - Japanese set meals. *Sets from 750 yen • 11am-11pm*
4) Hidakaya (日高屋) - ramen and gyoza dumplings. *Ramen from 390 yen • 10:30am-3:30pm*
5) Yoshinoya (吉野家) - gyudon and curry. *Bowls from 330 yen • 24h*
6) Sukiya (すき家) - gyudon and curry. *Bowls from 360 yen • 24h*
7) Tenya (天丼てんや) - tempura. *Bowls from 500 yen • 11am-11pm*
8) Wendy's First Kitchen (ファーストキッチン) - cheap soups, burgers and pasta. *Pasta from 580 yen, burgers from 370 yen • 5am-1am*

Local budget food

Best spots along Center Gai, in order from the station.
9) Yanbaru Okinawa Soba (やんばる 沖縄そば) - Set dishes and soba from Okinawa. *Noodles from 650 yen • 11am-11:30pm*
10) Yaro Ramen (野郎ラーメン) - Large sized ramen. *Ramen from 500 yen • 24h*
11) Kamukura Ramen (どうとんぼり神座) - Big menu, with English explanations on how to eat it and vegetarian options. *Ramen from 680 yen • 9am-8am*
12) Shakey's Pizza (シェーキーズ) - All-you-can-eat pizza restaurant, with Japanese and seasonal themed flavors. *Lunch time: adults 930 yen, teens 600 yen, under junior high school age 380 yen. Dinner time: 1540 yen, 1030 yen, 510 yen • 11am-11pm*
13) Okonomiyaki Mura (お好み焼むら) - All-you-can-eat Japanese pancakes, called Okonomiyaki. *90 mins for 1980 yen or Okonomiyaki from 780 yen • 4pm-2am*

Cheap supermarkets (スーパー)

Life Supermarket (ライフ渋谷東店) is a 10/15-minute walk away from Shibuya station on Meiji Dori, to the south and along the narrow river (9am-1am).

How to get there and away

From Shinjuku station, take the JR Yamanote Line to Shibuya station (6 mins, 150 yen). From Tokyo station, take the JR Yamanote Line to Shibuya station (24 mins, 190 yen). Also on Tokyo Metro **Fukutoshin**, **Hanzomon** and Ginza lines.
Recommended rail passes: Tokyo Subway Ticket, Tokyo Metro 24-hour Ticket, Tokyo Metropolitan District Pass

Tourist information (観光案内所)

Inside Shibuya station (in the Tokyu Line and Tokyo Metro Line area), on the second basement floor and near Miyamasuzaka Center exit (10am-7pm).

Harajuku (原宿)

Located between Shinjuku and Shibuya, Harajuku is the heartland of youth fashion and entertainment in Tokyo. It will provide plenty of splendid culture shock for a visitor, young or old. Many have heard the name Harajuku before, in popular culture or Japanese restaurant names, but it must really be seen to be believed. The area is full of independent boutiques and cafes, high-class shops and an increasing number of international chains, attracted by the status that being in Harajuku gives a brand.

Takeshita Dori, Harajuku

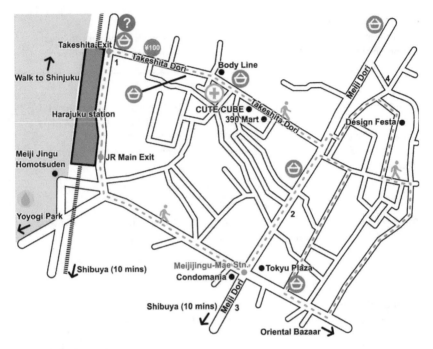

Walk it and save!

To see the real Harajuku, you can't just visit Takeshita Dori and Omotesando. There are some fascinating back streets and more chilled out areas seconds away. It's the best way to see what Japan's young (and young at heart) are up to. Use the walking route on the map to take you to all the highlights in Harajuku.

Things to do

Meiji Jingu

Meiji Jingu Shrine (明治神宮)

Located next to Yoyogi Park, Meiji Jingu is Tokyo's biggest and busiest Shinto shrine. Dedicated to the souls of Emperor Meiji and his consort Empress Shoken, the shrine is surrounded by a large forest, which contains more than 100,000 trees from all over Japan and overseas. The crowds do flock here, but the wide open paths and calm environment keep this place tranquil and peaceful. While one section of the forest requires a fee, it is completely free to visit the rest of it. Traditional Japanese weddings often take place in the shrine in the afternoon, so you may strike lucky! *FREE • Open at sunrise, closes at sundown (4-5pm) • Walk from Harajuku station, via wide bridge outside*

Homotsuden (Treasure Museum) (宝物殿)

Meiji Jingu has two treasure museums, for one entry fee. While it's not very popular with foreign tourists, the museums are an interesting insight into Japan's often forgotten history and its national treasures. Recent highlights include a 120 year old horse carriage used by a former emperor. *500 yen for both sites • 9am-4pm • Main building in north of park*

Takeshita Dori (竹下通)

A wonderful street filled with a variety of colorful and crazy fashions. Along the way you will see people shouting out special deals, offering great deals on everything from watches to shoes to bags. Even with all the cheap deals, this is not the main reason to come here. The street is full of very cute, very colorful Japanese shops that amaze even the most hardened tourists. The following highlights are in order as you approach from Harajuku station.

Daiso (ダイソー)

A big 100 yen discount store in Takeshita Dori Street. Get your drinks, cheap souvenirs and snacks here. *10am-9pm*

Bodyline

A treasure trove for anyone into cosplay or Lolita fashion, and an interesting peek into modern Japanese youth culture for others. Bodyline has prices starting from 200 yen for cute tights and decent boots can often be bought from around 3000 yen. Having said that, when there are clearance sales, shoes and tops can go from as low as 500 yen! *11am-8pm*

Cute Cube Harajuku

Small shopping mall full of unbelievably cute shops, such as a Sanrio shop for Hello Kitty goods and the adorable cafe with character-themed meals. Also has a branch of Chicago, for reasonably priced vintage clothes. *10am-8pm*

390 Mart (Thank You Mart)

If you say three, then nine in Japanese, the sound is "Sankyuu", similar to the English word "Thank you". As you may have guessed, everything here is only 390 yen. Kawaii (cute) socks, t-shirts, denim jeans and hats, plus a good selection of tote bags are available. *11am-8pm*

Yoyogi Park

A nice open park, great for playing games and sunbathing. Also one of Tokyo's most popular cherry blossom viewing areas. Come on Sunday for the Elvis dancers at the entrance! Cultural events and markets often take place here on the weekends in the summer, at the Yoyogi Outdoor Stage (代々木公園野外ステージ), just past the Yoyogi National Stadium. They usually have lots of stalls selling cheap Japanese food, as well as themed events, such as flea markets and food festivals. *FREE • 5am-8pm (until 5pm from mid Oct - Apr) • On the other side of Harajuku station*

Omotesando

While this street is well known to tourists, apart from a few exceptions it is definitely not a place for budget travelers to go shopping. Think more Burberry and Louis Vuitton than 100 yen discount stores. It is still worth a walk up though, as there are interesting shopping streets that head off from Omotesando and a few shops for foreign tourists:

Condomania (コンドマニア)

Yes, that's right, a shop dedicated to condoms. Its light-hearted and fun approach has given this shop quite a reputation. *11am-9:30pm • On the right hand side at first main junction, Metro exit 4*

Tokyu Plaza Omotesando Harajuku (東急プラザ)

New shopping mall, with a spectacular entrance of huge metallic mirrors. It says its aim is to become a fashion theme park, and Tokyu Plaza certainly does a good job of spicing up shopping with a bunch of quirky shops. Grab a drink somewhere cheaper and chill out on the top, a super trendy rooftop garden looking over Harajuku. *10am-9pm • On left hand side after first main junction, opposite Condomania •* http://omohara.tokyu-plaza.com/en/

Oriental Bazaar (オリエンタルバザアー)

One of the best souvenir shops in Japan. They have reasonably priced yukatas (traditional Japanese gowns) for sale and about any kind of gift you could want to take back. Staff are also very useful if you don't understand how things work or what their purpose is. *10am-7pm • Continue down Omotesando, a minute after first junction, on right •* http://www.orientalbazaar.co.jp/

Design Festa Gallery (デザインフェスタギャラリー)

A host of small galleries, more than 70 when at full capacity, showing off the latest up-and-coming artists. All sorts of styles, and ever changing exhibitions on display. Design Festa has become a bit of an institution in Harajuku, and makes going to an expensive gallery unnecessary for most. *FREE • Times vary by gallery • After walking down Takeshita Dori from Harajuku station, cross the road and continue forward. Take the second left, it's on the right side •* http://www.designfestagallery.com/index_en.html

Budget food

It's a bit difficult to find cheap food in Harajuku, so definitely stick with the cheap chain restaurants and convenience stores, or see what is on offer in Yoyogi Park.

Budget restaurants on map

1) Yoshinoya (吉野家) - gyudon and curry. *Bowls from 330 yen • 24h*
2) Tempura Tenya (天丼てんや) - deep-fried fish and vegetables. *Bowls from 500 yen • 11am-11pm*

Local budget food

3) Ichiran Ramen (一蘭) - Ramen bar that focuses on Tonkotsu (pork) based ramen, and does it pretty damned well. *Ramen from 790 yen • 7am-11:30pm • Walk down Omotesando from Harajuku station, then take a right at first junction and look for 一蘭 characters on other side (opposite Metro exit 7)*
4) Nagaraya Bento (ながらや) - Pick up a posher than usual bento at this local shop. *Bento boxes from 680 yen • 10am-5pm • Cross road at end of Takeshita Dori (if coming from Harajuku station), walk down narrow street on left for 2 mins*

Cheap supermarkets (スーパー)

There are no supermarkets, but plenty of large convenience stores around.

Water bottle refill spots

There are some water fountains in Yoyogi Park, but it could be quite a trek just to refill your bottle. Head to Daiso for cheap drinks and snacks.

Pharmacy (ドラッグストア)

Matsukiyo (薬 マツモトキヨシ) has a pharmacy down Takeshita Dori (9:30am - 10pm).

How to get there and away

By rail

From Shinjuku station, take the JR Yamanote Line to Harajuku station (4 mins, 130 yen). From Tokyo station, take the JR Yamanote Line to Harajuku station (26 mins, 190 yen). If using the Metro, head to Meijijingu-Mae station on the Fukutoshin or Chiyoda lines. *Recommended rail passes: Tokyo Subway Ticket, Tokyo Metro 24-hour Ticket, Tokyo Metropolitan District Pass*

Walk it and save!

To/from Shinjuku, we have walked the distance in under 30 minutes. The best route is to go via the grounds of Meiji Jingu, which has an entrance at the south near Harajuku station and another in the north near Shinjuku station. Most visitors will go around these grounds anyway, so it's a worthwhile money saving idea. Just stay on the west side of the JR Yamanote Line (look out for the trains with light green lines on them) tracks and you will get to your destination.

Tourist information (観光案内所)

H.I.S has an unofficial, but still very helpful tourist information center (10am-5:30pm), a little further north from the entrance to Takeshita Dori if coming from Harajuku station.

Koenji (高円寺)

Koenji, like Shimo-Kitazawa, is a trendy town with many cheap shops, cafes, bars and restaurants. Known as Tokyo's main counter-culture area, it features some great second-hand book and music shops. A great place to escape the tourist crowds of Shinjuku and Shibuya, Koenji is often a favorite spot for foreigners living, rather than just traveling, in Tokyo.

Things to do

The best way to experience Koenji is to walk around the station, up the various shopping streets, looking for some bargains. Koenji is really a great place for a spot of window shopping, and purchasing a few interesting goods. The counter-culture vibe has also helped to develop some great independent, but not too pricey, restaurants and take-out shops.

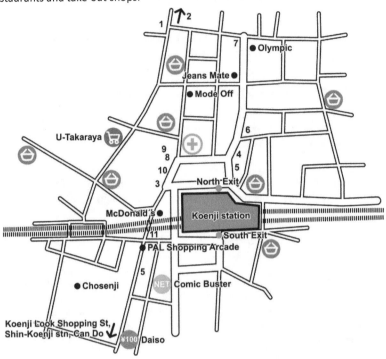

Chosenji Temple (長仙寺)

Not essential, as this is a rather small and not so impressive temple, but if you want a quick break from walking around it does make for a relaxing spot. *FREE • 24h • Head right after St. Marc Cafe down PAL Shopping Arcade (高円寺パル商店街)*

Shopping

Looking for cheap clothes? Second-hand or recycled goods? Cute but stylish accessories or ornaments? Koenji is going to blow your socks off if you are into these things. Countless independent shops sell all sorts of goods, so give yourself at least an hour or two to explore.

South of Koenji station

PAL Shopping Arcade (高円寺パル商店街)

An interesting spot for a bit of shopping, PAL has more chains than elsewhere, but still has a few gems. Village Vanguard (ヴィレッジヴァンガード) is an iconic, crazy shop full of random 'only in Japan' items, magazines and posters to take home (10am-midnight) and the game arcade has plenty of 100 yen games to play. *Take the south exit from Koenji station, then take a right turn and walk a little until you see the PAL sign above.*

Koenji Look Shopping Street (高円寺ルック商店街)

Lined with second-hand and antique stores, plus some funky cafes and tiny up-and-coming restaurants. Prices may be higher than the 100 yen shops, but there are some real bargains to be found. If buying lots, don't be afraid to haggle, even though this is Japan! *Continue on from PAL Shopping Arcade or start at Shin-Koenji (Metro Marunouchi Line) and walk up.*

North of Koenji station

Olympic (オリンピック)

Cheap bicycles, everyday essentials and basic fashion items at not too bad a price. *10am-9pm • Once out of Koenji station (north exit), head down the road with the orange Yoshinoya restaurant*

Jeans Mate (ジーンズメイト)

Yes, the information below is correct, this is a 24 hour jean shop. Cheap T-shirts, shoes and of course jeans, plus tax-free available for foreign tourists (remember your passport). *24h • Opposite Olympic*

Mode Off (モードオフ)

Second-hand and retro clothes, bags, hats and accessories available in this large store. *11am-9pm • Head out of Koenji station (north exit), head up the street with the Sundrug (サンドラッグ高円寺店)*

100 yen shops

Daiso (ダイソー) - A little small, but has all the 100 yen essentials. *10am-9pm*
Can Do (キャンドゥイ) - Much larger choice than Daiso, with a good selection on everyday essentials. *10am-9pm • All the way down Koenji Look Shopping Street.*

Pharmacy (ドラッグストア)

Sundrug (サンドラッグ高円寺店) has a huge shop across from Koenji station, north exit (10am-10:45pm).

Budget food

1) Sempre Pizza (センプレ ピッツァ) - We don't know how this place keeps things so cheap, but they sell real Italian pizzas for only a few coins. *Pizzas from 350 yen • 11:30am-10pm • Head out of Koenji station (north exit), head up the street with the Sundrug (サンドラッグ高円寺店), take a left at the end and walk down*
2) Floresta Nature Doughnuts (フロレスタ高円寺店) - Fancy doughnuts and some good choices for those who want a healthier, organic sweet snack. *Doughnuts from 150 yen • 9am-9pm • From Sempre Pizza, take a right turn and walk up the street*
3) Mister Donut (ミスタードーナツ) - Cheaper option for doughnuts, with a huge choice. Also sells cheap snacks like sausage rolls, soups and breads. *Doughnuts from 100 yen, breads from 120 yen • 7am-11pm • Near McDonald's at Koenji station, north exit*
4) Yoshinoya (吉野家) - Gyudon eat-in and takeaway. *Meals from 330 yen • 24h • North exit of Koenji station*

5) Kaiten Misakiko (海鮮三崎港) - Some of the cheapest sushi in Tokyo, and great quality. *Sushi plate from 110 yen + tax • 11am-11pm • One branch is outside Koenji station (north exit), on the right next to Yoshinoya. The other is a minute down PAL Shopping Arcade*

6) Hotto Motto (ほっともっと) - Another good bento spot in Koenji, with a more varied menu than Origin Bento. *Bento boxes from 390 yen • 8am-11pm • From Koenji station (north exit), walk a little past Yoshinoya on the right. Hotto Motto is on the right side*

7) Origin Bento - The most popular bento chain in Tokyo, we have forgotten the number of times we have visited this Koenji branch. *Bento boxes from 390 yen • 24h • Head out of Koenji station (north exit) up the street with the Sundrug (サンドラッグ高円寺店), take a right at the end and walk down two blocks*

8) Matsuya (松屋) - Gyudon and burger eat-in and takeaway. *Meals from 290 yen • 24h • On the left side after exiting Koenji station, north exit*

9) Bochi Bochi Okonomiyaki (ぼちぼち) - Reasonably priced okonomiyaki (Japanese pancake) restaurant. *Plates from 800 yen • 11am-11pm • Just above Matsuya*

10) Tenya Tempura (天丼てんや) - Cheap tempura bowls and plates. *Bowls from 500 yen • 11am-11:30pm • On the left side after exiting Koenji station, north exit*

11) Kyotaru Sushi (京樽) - Cheap sushi stall, with discounts in the evenings before closing. *Sushi boxes from 490 yen • 9am-10pm • Behind McDonald's, outside Koenji station, north exit*

Cheap supermarkets (スーパー)

There is a cheap supermarket called U-Takaraya (ユータカラヤ) near the north exit (10am-9am).

Nightlife

There are a host of cheap outside bars around the station, and under the tracks, especially on the left as you exit on the north side. We recommend having a walk around and seeing which one you like the look of. There are also some yakitori restaurants around here as well, but be careful with ordering, as the prices can go sky high if you get more than a few sticks.

Free wifi locations

Wifi reception is awful in Koenji station, so head outside to get on the net. McDonald's, just to the left of the north exit, has good wifi.

How to get there and away

From Shinjuku station, take the Chuo Line or Sobu Line to Koenji station (6 mins, 150 yen). From Tokyo station, take the Chuo Line to Koenji station (20 mins, 200 yen). You need to change at Nakano station on weekends. *Recommended rail passes: Tokyo Metropolitan District Pass, Tokyo Subway Ticket, Tokyo Metro 24-hour Ticket. If using a subway pass, go to Shin-Koenji station on the Marunouchi Line, and walk north up Koenji Look Shopping Street (高円寺ルック商店街).*

Kichijoji (吉祥寺)

Kichijoji is a nice place to spend a cheap day, just walking around and doing an odd bit of shopping, eating or relaxing in the park. It's the most interesting suburban area outside central Tokyo, and has many things to keep all types of people occupied. Kichijoji is well worth spending an afternoon in with its blend of local bargains and less crowded tourist spots.

Walk it and save!

Kichijoji is all walkable on foot, another reason it's great for budget travelers. It can be a bit confusing to know where exactly you are, so use the landmarks on the map to help you out. Use the recommended walking route to help you out. When you get to the park, leave from the other exit, as shown in the map:

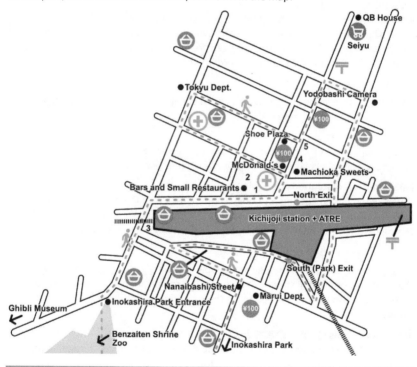

Things to do

Inokashira Park

Inokashira Park is a great place to come during the cherry blossom season or during the autumn colors. Other times, it is a relaxing spot for a stroll, especially on weekends with impromptu flea market stalls selling inventive goods and performers doing all kinds of free performances by the lake. *FREE • 24h • Short walk south of Kichijoji station*

Ghibli Museum (三鷹の森ジブリ美術館)

A house full of the same kind of magic that makes Ghibli films so great, the building looks like it was taken off a set of one of the movies. Original artwork, playrooms and a cinema showing short films, plus a special exhibition every year. Note that you cannot buy tickets on the day. Check the Ghibli Museum for how to buy tickets or go to a Lawson convenience store to buy beforehand (ask the staff for help). *Ages 19 and over 1000 yen, Ages 13 to 18 700 yen, Ages 7 to 12 400 yen, Ages 4 to 6 100 yen • 10am-6pm • Well signposted from park • http://www.ghibli-museum.jp/en/*

Benzaiten Shrine

A beautiful shrine on a little island in the park. Benzaiten is a Japanese Buddhist goddess, based on the Hindu goddess Saraswati. The shrine therefore has a few touches from both religions. *FREE • 24h*

Inokashira Park Zoo

A reasonably priced zoo with a good selection of animals and birds. Nothing too crazy in here, but if you like animals (and have children to entertain) it's worth it. *Adults 400 yen (FREE with Grutto Pass), Children (13-15) 150 yen, Children (12 and under) FREE • 9:30am-5pm (closed on Monday)*

North of Kichijoji station

There are all sorts of businesses here, such as cheap clothes shops, nice restaurants and occasional 'pop-up' food stalls.

Yodobashi Camera

A huge, huge electronics store, and without the crowds of Akihabara or Shinjuku. Tax-free shopping available. *9:30am-10pm • Up the wide road from the north exit*

Bars and small restaurants

Opposite the Baskin Robbins ice cream shop to the left of the north exit, be sure to explore this unique area. Most of the bars are a little expensive, but it has lots of atmosphere with its small narrow lanes packed with bars and restaurants.

Sun Road (吉祥寺サンロード商店街)

Great place to start your shopping and people watching in Kichijoji. Head out from the north exit of Kichijoji station. Sun Road is the roofed shopping arcade with the McDonald's. Also be sure to head off to the many interesting roads and side paths along it.

Machioka Sweets (おかしのまちおか)

A treasure trove of Japanese candy and soda drinks, this charming shop often has great deals to entice people in, like drinks for 60 yen or candy value multipacks. *10am-9pm*

100 yen shops

Pack your bags with $1 drinks, gifts, snacks and more at Daiso (ダイソー) or CanDo (キャン・ドゥ). *10am-9pm*

Shoe Plaza (シュープラザ)

Bargain shoe superstore, one of many you will see around these Kichijoji shopping arcades. *10am-9pm*

QB House

1000 yen haircutters. Get yourself the cheapest haircut of your life (and quickest, at under 10 minutes), or have a peek in at the huge vacuums they use to quickly suck up the hair on the floor! *1000 yen per cut • 10am-10pm • Under Seiyu Supermarket*

Nanaibashi Street (七井橋通り)

A really cool shopping street with loads of trendy shops and fancy cafes, so worth checking out to see what daily life is like in Kichijoji. Not generally the best place to get any bargains, but you may come across a sale or two if you're lucky! *Head south from Kichijoji. Nanaibashi Street is down the side of Marui Department Store.*

Budget food

1) Fuji Soba (富士そば) - No frills soba and udon bar, with small curries and other side dishes. *Soba from 290 yen • 24h • Opposite Baskin Robbins, near the north exit*
2) Hamonika Quina (ハモニカ・クイナ) - Tacorice is a famous Okinawa invention, combining Japanese rice with a topping of what would be a filling to a Mexican taco. This one is the best in Tokyo. *Tacorice from 690 yen • 11:30am-10pm • In collection of small bars and restaurants opposite Baskin Robbins, from the north exit*
3) Sempre Pizza (センプレ ピッツァ) - Super cheap, tasty pizzas. *Pizzas from 350 yen • 10am-9pm • Just outside the Atre shopping mall east exit*
4) Shakey's (シェーキーズ) - All-you-can-eat pizza restaurant, with Japanese and seasonal themed flavors. Expect to be surprised by this imaginative menu! *Lunch time: adults 1160 yen, teens 880 yen, under junior high school age 500 yen. Dinner time: 1650 yen, 1000 yen, 500 yen • 11am-10:15pm • On Sun Road*
5) Matsuya (松屋) - Gyudon and burger eat-in and takeaway. *Meals from 290 yen • 24h • Half way down Sun Road*

Cheap supermarkets (スーパー)

Seiyu has a huge supermarket towards the end of Sun Road (10am-11pm).

Pharmacy (ドラッグ ストア)

Sundrug (サンドラッグ サンロード店) is on Sun Road (10am - 10:15pm).

How to get there and away

From Shinjuku station, take the JR Chuo Line to Kichijoji station (210 yen, 15 mins). From other stations, first get to Shinjuku station. If using a Tokyo Metropolitan District Pass, you need to pay from Nishi-Ogikubo to Kichijoji (140 yen).

Meguro and Ebisu (目黒と恵比寿)

Well known to expats and fashionable Japanese, Meguro and Ebisu are not tourist hotspots, but places that everyday people love to hang out at. While 20-somethings go to Shibuya or Harajuku, these areas cater to more sophisticated and quieter tastes. Some restaurants and bars can therefore be a bit expensive, but if you follow the tips below you will be able to enjoy a budget day away from the crowds.

Things to do

Meguro

Meguro Parasitological Museum (目黒寄生虫館)

The Meguro Parasitological Museum is a truly 'only in Japan' experience! This museum is dedicated to bugs, parasites and other creepy crawlies. It claims to be the only such museum in the world, and the experience is definitely not a standard touristy one. Be prepared to be both shocked and amazed! Especially at the nine meter long tape-worm taken from one rather unfortunate victim. *FREE • 10am-5pm (closed Mondays and Tuesdays or the following day if these are national holidays) • From Meguro station, head west along Meguro Dori, crossing over a large bridge. Walk up until you get to a Royal Host restaurant on your right. The museum is a little further on, across the road*

Institute for Nature Study, National Museum of Nature and Science

Need to get back into nature, and quick? This surprisingly unknown forest in the heart of Tokyo is a great spot for an easy woodland walk or a spot of bird watching. A true sanctuary for natural beauty and birdlife, the mixed forest is easy to navigate. *310 yen • 9am-5pm (closed Mondays) • 10-minute walk along Meguro Dori from the east exit of JR Meguro station*

Naka-Meguro

While this area has a reputation for being expensive and upper-class, Meguro River (目黒川) is a cool place to chill out in the evening with a drink or two. There are convenience stores around if you want to buy cheap beer or a bento to save on cash. Naka-Meguro is particularly popular during the cherry blossom season, when the river is lined with sakura trees. *Naka-Meguro station or 10-minute walk down main road from Ebisu, heading west*

Ebisu

Museum of Yebisu Beer (エビスビール記念館)

Mainly known as Ebisu Beer, one of the top three beer brands in Japan. The museum features a good number of displays on the history of Yebisu Beer, as well as Japanese beer in general. The Tasting Salon (reasonable fees apply) is the highlight here, and the shop features everything from branded beer jugs to beer jelly. *FREE • 11am-7pm (closed Mondays and New Year holidays) • Once at Ebisu station follow the signs to the museum (5 minutes on foot)*

Budget food

Around the stations are the usual budget chains, but most of the spots of interest are away from the stations, so consider eating before visiting these.

Cheap supermarkets (スーパー)

There is a 24h Maruetsu (マルエツ) supermarket on the way to the Meguro Parasitological Museum, as well as some smaller ones in and around the stations. Tokyu Store, just outside Meguro station's west exit is good (10am-11pm).

100 yen shops
Can Do (キャンドゥイ) - Inside the Tokyu Store. *10am-10pm*

How to get there and away

Meguro
On the JR Yamanote Line, Metro **Namboku Line** and Toei **Mita Line**. From Shibuya, take the JR Yamanote Line to Meguro station (160 yen, 5 mins).

Ebisu
One more stop on the JR Yamanote Line from Meguro. Also on JR Shonan-Shinjuku Line, JR **Saikyo** Line and Metro **Hibiya** Line. *Recommended rail passes: Tokyo Subway Ticket, Tokyo Metro 24-hour Ticket, Tokyo Metropolitan District Pass*

Shimo-Kitazawa (下北沢)

Shimo-Kitazawa is a trendy district with plenty of second-hand shops, bars, record shops, interesting fashions and nice cafes and restaurants. If you are into buying cheap clothes, CDs or ornaments, Shimo-Kitazawa is a must. While tourists tend to flock to the main areas of Shibuya and Shinjuku, 'Shimo' is where residents go to hang out and do a bit of budget shopping. It's where all the cool, young people go!

Shopping and other things to do

The best way to experience Shimo-Kitazawa is to walk around randomly and just soak it in. The streets are so narrow and numerous, so don't worry too much about getting lost. Just enjoy walking down any street that looks interesting and you should come across some nice spots. There are too many discount, thrift and second-hand stores to list them all, so here are some highlights. There are many more between these and down nearby side streets.

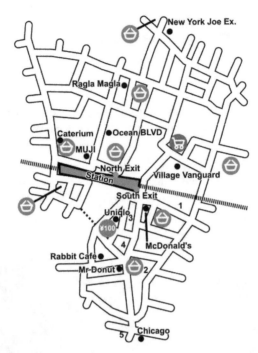

Ocean BLVD (古着屋 Ocean BLVD)

More than a dozen small shops selling cheap clothes, souvenirs, ornaments, retro toys and much more. The tightly packed-in shops are all independent ones, which gives the place a slightly chaotic but fun atmosphere. *11am-8pm*

Ragla Magla

All clothing items and accessories are 990 yen at this shore, from blouses to bags to coats. They also have further occasional deals, such as the completely nuts 2980 yen 'all you can pack in your shopping basket' sale. *12am-9pm*

New York Joe Exchange

Located in a former public bathhouse, this store has a good selection of very cheap, but good quality clothing from a variety of brands. The staff are also very knowledgeable about current fashions and are super helpful. First Sunday of every month also has a 50% off everything sale. *12am-8pm • Continue down the road from Ocean BLVD, take right at Lawson convenience store. It's on the left side*

Village Vanguard (ヴィレッジヴァンガード)

Another branch of the crazy pack-em-in variety store. This one is great for funny souvenirs, full of 'only in Japan' items as well as books and amusing costumes. Worth a visit even if you have absolutely no money to spend on shopping. *10am-midnight*

Chicago (シカゴ)

The largest branch in Tokyo of this used clothing store. Chicago has a load of reasonably priced clothing, from international brands to local vintage ones. They also have a large selection of used kimonos, yukatas, obi (traditional belts), Japanese slippers and related accessories. *11am-8pm*

Caterium (キャットカフェ キャテリアム)

Chilled out cafe, with the difference being all the cats walking about! Visitors can dress up the cats in all sorts of cute clothing, or have a play using plenty of adorable toys. *1 hour 1000 yen (includes one drink) • 11am-9pm • From the north exit, head left and up past Muji. Take a right, and Caterium is just above 7-Eleven*

Rabbit Cafe Ohisama (うさぎ Cafe おひさま)

While cat cafes are the most popular animal cafes in Tokyo, this smaller cafe is infested with another cute variety of animal. There are also clothes to put on the rabbits (try the kimono!) or you can have fun feeding or stroking them. *30 mins 1000 yen (includes one drink) • 12pm-8pm • From the south exit, walk down the shopping street with McDonald's on its left. At Mister Donut, walk a bit down the narrow street on the right (on right side, 2F)*

Uniqlo (ユニクロ)

A quieter branch of Japan's most popular cheap clothes shop chain. *10am-9pm*

100 yen shops

Daiso (ダイソー) - Daiso has a good shop in the small shopping mall of the above Uniqlo. *10am-9pm*

Getting around

You will get lost here, at least once, but don't worry as it's part of the charm of Shimo-Kitazawa. If you get lost, use the map and try to retrace your steps using the various landmarks. If all is lost, head back to the station ("eki" in Japanese) and walk around it until you get to your desired station exit. It's all very walkable.

Budget food

Apart from some chain restaurants, there are other cheap options available for food in Shimo-Kitazawa, but most budget travelers should head to Oseki supermarket.

1) CONA - Delicious 'one coin' pizzas, but in a stylish, laidback setting. Note that after 5pm there is a 300 yen cover charge, so come at lunch. *Pizzas from 500 yen • 12am-11pm*

2) Hiroki - Hiroshima style okonomiyaki (Japanese pancake) restaurant, possibly the best in Tokyo. This style has soba or udon inside the okonomiyaki. *Okonomiyaki from 900 yen • 12am-9:45pm • Continue down from CONA, head right at the first intersection, then walk a minute down*

3) Matsuya (松屋) - Gyudon and burger eat-in and takeaway. *Meals from 290 yen • 24h*

4) Hidakaya Ramen (日高屋) - Tokyo's super cheap ramen chain. Fried rice and gyoza dumplings also available. There are also slightly more expensive, but more authentic ramen joints on the same street. *Ramen from 390 yen • 24h*

5) Ohsho (餃子の王将) - Chinese inspired ramen, fried rice and gyoza dumpling chain with a large, English menu. *Ramen from 500 yen, dumplings from 240 yen • 11:30am-4am*

Cheap supermarkets (スーパー)

Oseki (オオゼキ) is a particularly good supermarket for cheap sushi. Also has a variety of cheap bento boxes, snacks and drinks (9:30am-6pm). Take a left from the south exit and walk down to the end.

Pharmacy (ドラッグストア)

There are several around the station. An easy one to get to is Ippondo Drug Store (ドラッグストア 一本堂), near Vanguard (10am-10pm).

How to get there and away

From Shinjuku, take the Odakyu Line to Shimo-Kitazawa station (7 mins, 150 yen). From Shibuya, take the Keio Inokashira Line to Shimo-Kitazawa (6 mins, 120 yen).

Ueno (上野)

Ueno features one of the biggest parks in Tokyo and is one of the main 'cities' within the megalopolis that is Tokyo. There are many museums in the park, and the area is full of brightly lit streets and stores. While it has branches of the main electronic and clothing mega stores, visitors should head to Ameyoko and the park to see what makes Ueno different.

Ameyoko market, Ueno

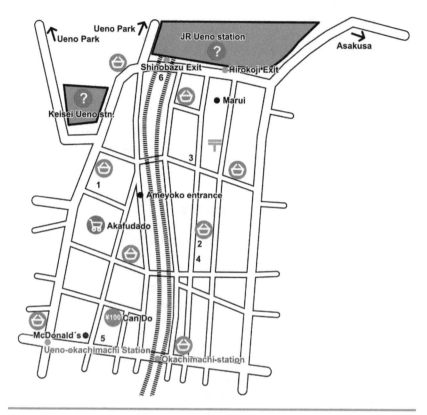

Things to do

Ameyoko (アメ横)

A fascinating collection of streets with many street vendors, Japanese restaurants and game arcades. The atmosphere certainly gets lively here at the weekends, with traders shouting out deals, trying to beat their rivals to get that all important sale. Everything is on sale here of course, such as discount candy, dried fruits, handbags, perfume and watches. Traders will sometimes give you a good bargain, if you are nice! *Take the Shinobazu exit from JR Ueno and follow signs*

Can Do 100 yen store (キャンドゥ イ)

Walk down Ameyoko and head left at the crossroads with ABC Mart. *10am-9pm*

Ueno park

A huge park, and known as a great place to view the cherry blossoms. Apart from the museums and zoo, free highlights include Bentendo (7am-5pm), an octagonal temple hall, and Toshogu Shrine (9am-4:30pm). Maps are located all over the park, so getting around is easy. *To get there, use the Koen (Park) exit of Ueno station and walk over the road.*

Ueno Zoo (上野動物園)

Tokyo's largest and by far the most popular zoo, especially good for children, but also fun for adults. This is the park containing the famous pandas from China, so be prepared to line up! *Adults 600 yen, children 200 yen, under 12s FREE • 9:30am-5pm (closed Mondays) • West side of park*

Tokyo National Museum (東京国立博物館)

The first stop for anyone with a keen interest in Japanese history, art, design or fashion. It's the oldest national museum in Japan and has by far the richest variety of exhibitions. With more than 110,000 objects and 87 national treasures, you will need at least a few hours to explore the whole complex. *Adults 620 yen, under-18s and over-70s FREE • 9:30am-5pm (closed Mondays and New Year holidays) • North side of park*

Tokyo Metropolitan Art Museum (東京都美術館)

A prefectural art museum, largely built underground so as not to stand out too much in the green park. The temporary shows have a vast range of art from across the world, from Van Gogh to Japanese calligraphy. *FREE for main exhibitions • 9:30am-5:30pm (closed every first and third Monday) • North west side of park*

National Museum of Nature and Science (国立科学博物館)

Split into a Japan Gallery and a Global Gallery, this museum thankfully has English explanations for large number of exhibits. As well as having standard exhibitions on dinosaurs and nature, visitors can also learn about the history of humans in Japan and the ecologically diverse islands. Definitely recommended for children, especially as they get in for free. *Adults 620 yen, children FREE • 9am-5pm (closed Mondays and New Year holidays) • East side of park*

National Museum of Western Art (国立西洋美術館)

Now a World Heritage Site, this museum was designed by Frenchman Le Corbusier in 1959, an influential architect known for heavily influencing 20th century architecture around the world. The museum itself has ever changing exhibitions, so have a peek inside to see if they are of interest to you. *Adults 430 yen, children FREE • 9:30am-5:30pm (closed Mondays and New Year holidays) • East side of park*

Travel discounts and packages

The Grutto Pass gives FREE access to the zoo, 100 yen off at The Ueno Royal Museum, 80 yen off The National Museum of Western Art, 100 yen off Tokyo National Museum and 100 yen off special exhibitions at Tokyo Metropolitan Art Museum.

Budget food

Budget restaurants on map

1) Matsuya (松屋) - rice bowls and curry. *Gyudon bowls from 290 yen • 24h*
2) Ringer Hut (リンガーハット) - fish ramen. *Ramen from 630 yen • 10am-2am*
3) Fujisan Sushi (すし富士山) - conveyor belt sushi. *Sushi from 140 yen • 11:30am-11:20pm*

4) Hidakaya (日高屋) - ramen and gyoza dumplings. *Ramen from 390 yen • 10am-3am*

5) Yoshinoya (吉野家) - gyudon and curry. *Bowls from 330 yen • 24h*

6) Tsuruya (つるや) - cheap soba and udon. *Soba from 290 yen • 4:30am-1am*

Ameyoko

There are lots of small stalls and shops selling fruits, ice creams and deep fried snacks for 100-300 yen each. Larger takeout meals (such as Japanese pancakes, kebabs and noodles) are around 400-500 yen, so this is a great spot for budget travelers. Be sure to explore the interconnecting streets for a few gems and special offers as well.

Cheap supermarkets (スーパー)

Akafudado (赤札堂) has a branch in the AbAb (アブアブ) shopping mall (10am-9pm). Note that Ameyoko also has plenty of stalls selling basic items like fruits, vegetables and cheap takeouts.

Water bottle refill spots

The park has some water fountains, or go to the chain restaurants.

Pharmacy (ドラッグストア)

Plenty of drug stores are open late on Ameyoko.

How to get there and away

From Shinjuku station, take the JR Yamanote Line to Ueno station (25 mins, 190 yen). From Tokyo station, take the JR Yamanote Line to Ueno station (6 mins, 150 yen). Ueno is also on the Tokyo Metro Hibiya and Ginza lines. *Recommended rail passes: Tokyo Subway Ticket, Tokyo Metro 24-hour Ticket, Tokyo Metropolitan District Pass*

Walk it and save!

Asakusa is a nice city walk from Ueno, via Kappabashi. We recommend starting with Ueno in the morning, then strolling over to Asakusa in the early evening/late afternoon. Check the map for the road to go down. After about 30 minutes you will get to Asakusa.

Tourist information (観光案内所)

Both JR Ueno stations (9:15am-5:15pm) and Keisei Ueno stations (9:30am-6:30pm) have tourist information centers. Ueno Park also has a small information booth near Ueno Royal Museum.

Imperial Palace area (皇居東御苑と東京駅)

Hama Rikyu Garden, near the Imperial Palace

While the area around Tokyo station is expensive real estate, with shop and restaurant prices to reflect that, there are some essential stops for budget travelers. The Imperial Palace East Garden is a highlight for many in Tokyo, and there are a few other free spots to check out in the area. Just forget that the land value of the area used to be more valuable than the whole of California's, take in the modern city sights and take plenty of photos.

Travel discounts and packages

Tokyo Station Area Art Gallery Map (東京駅周辺美術館共通券)
Get 100 yen off at five galleries around Tokyo station. Just pick up the map from one of the galleries or the information center and bring it with you to each one. The discounts work at Tokyo Station Gallery, Bridgestone Museum of Art, Idemitsu Museum of Arts, Mitsui Memorial Museum and Mitsubishi Ichigokan Museum. Also consider the Grutto Pass, though, if you want to see even more than these ones.

Things to do

Tokyo station

Imperial Palace East Garden (皇居東御苑)
The East Garden, right in the center of Tokyo, is a free park within the Imperial Palace complex. First opened to the public in 1968, the 210,000 square meters garden has a variety of interesting spots. Highlights include the Honmaru castle

compound, one of the last remaining Edo period gardens in Ninomaru, and the remains of the former castle tower. The free Museum of the Imperial Collections (Sannomaru-Shōzōkan) contains 9,500 items of Imperial art, such as paintings and calligraphy artifacts. *FREE • 9am-4:30pm (closed Monday and Friday) • Near Otemachi station exit C10, which is connected to Tokyo station by underground passage*

Tokyo Character Street (東京キャラクターストリート)

Plenty of free samples to be had here. This underground shopping mall has more than 20 stores, all themed after well-known characters in Japanese comics, manga, games, music and on TV. They have everyone covered, from Hello Kitty to Rilakkuma to Doraemon. There is also a pop-up shop area called 'Ichiban Plaza', which has various themed stalls open. *FREE • 10am-10:30pm • Near JR Tokyo station Yaesu Underground central exit and Daimaru Dept. Store*

Walk it and save!

The most famous walking or jogging route for any Tokyoite is to go around the whole grounds of the Imperial Palace. It's a pretty simple, flat route and the scenery along the way is a perfect mix of tall skyscrapers, greenery and downtown city life. Start by walking from the west side of Tokyo station, and once you get to the moat just head around in either direction. *Time required: 2 hours • Difficulty: Easy*

Shimbashi

Hama Rikyu Garden (浜離宮)

Japan's premier garden, you may not need to visit another after this one. The garden has two parts, the southern part which was a villa for feudal lords in the 17th to 19th centuries and the more modern northern garden. On the south end, an area originally used as hunting grounds for the shogun ruler of Japan has been reborn. Now Shio-iri-no Niwa, it's a splendid Japanese garden on the sea, and also has a waterbus to Asakusa and Odaiba. *300 yen • 9am-5pm • From Shimbashi, follow signs to Shiodome, then to the garden (behind Conrad Tokyo hotel / コンラッド東京)*

Advertising Museum Tokyo (アド・ミュージアム) (reopening December 2017)

A surprisingly interesting (and free!) museum, showcasing Japanese advertising over the centuries. From Kimono ladies selling beer to retro packaging, the museum is a fascinating change from the usual museums in Tokyo. *FREE • 11am-6:30pm (until 4:30pm Saturdays. Closed Saturdays, Mondays and holidays) • Take the subway to Shiodome station (Oedo Line) or Shimbashi (JR Yamanote, Ginza and Asakusa Metro Lines). From these, follow the signs underground to the museum*

Budget food

Tokyo station itself, plus the area around is mainly filled up with overpriced restaurants and bakeries. It's therefore highly recommended to eat elsewhere or bring food with you. Shimbashi is a similar case, but there are a few chain restaurants outside the station if you are desperate to sit down and eat. Otherwise head straight to the convenience stores for a cheap bento or cup noodle.

Water bottle refill spots

There are occasional water fountains in the parks and gardens, or you can refill in one of the chain restaurants.

Pharmacy (ドラッグストア)

There is a Matsumoto-Kiyoshi pharmacy (マツモトキヨシ) in the Yaesu underground mall (8am-9pm).

How to get there and away

There are more than a dozen JR and Metro lines to Tokyo station, so check at your nearest station for the quickest route. For Shimbashi, take the JR Yamanote Line (140 yen, 4 mins) from Tokyo station. Shimbashi is also on the Tokyo Metro Asakusa and Ginza lines. *Recommended rail passes: Tokyo Subway Ticket, Tokyo Metro 24-hour Ticket, Tokyo Metropolitan District Pass*

Tourist information (観光案内所)

There is a TIC Tokyo center in Marunouchi Trust Tower, just to the right after using the Nihonbashi exit (10am-7pm).

Asakusa (浅草)

Asakusa is the main tourist zone in Tokyo, a bustling area full of tourists from across the world. While this may put some travelers off, it is still a must see for any first time visitor to Japan. Asakusa features Tokyo's most famous temple, atmospheric old-fashioned streets and plenty of free things to do for budget travelers.

So the map is easy to read, convenience stores have not been included

There is both a Tobu Asakusa station, as well as the combined Tokyo Metro and Toei Subway underground section. To get your bearings from the underground, head for exit 1,2 or 3, which all bring you out on Kaminarimon Dori (street), the main street on the map.

Things to do

Asakusa

Senso-ji Temple (浅草寺)

Tokyo's most famous and popular temple. One of the oldest in Tokyo, founded in 628. The Asakusa Kannon deity (goddess of mercy) was enshrined here, so many believe visiting the temple will bring good fortune to all. Be sure to walk around the whole complex, including the five-storey pagoda, as there is lots to see apart from the main buildings. Walking around the temple complex in the evening is also rather impressive. *FREE • Grounds 24h, main hall 6am-5pm (until 6:30pm Oct - Mar) • Through Kaminarimon and down five mins*

Kaminarimon (雷門)

Get your selfie stick out for Tokyo's premier selfie spot. The 'Thunder Gate' features statues of Raijin, god of thunder, and Fujin, god of wind. The giant lantern hanging below is probably the most photographed in Japan. *FREE • Down Kaminarimon Dori from Asakusa (Tokyo Metro) station exits 1,2,3*

Nakamise Street (仲見世通り)

Asakusa is full of interesting shops for a bit of window shopping and the occasional purchase! Many of the streets look like Tokyo of the past. Take your time here, as you may be able to watch stall owners make traditional Japanese sweets, such as Ningyoyaki (Japanese snack cakes), which you can buy for 100 yen or so after. As this is the main tourist destination in Tokyo, prices can be high around the main temple and nearby streets. There are plenty of cheaper spots outside this main tourist zone. *Between Kaminarimon and Senso-ji Temple*

Sumida Park and River (墨田公園・墨田川)

A quiet park along the river, and a good place to chill out for a bit or enjoy a bento. A must see during the cherry blossom season. *East of Asakusa station*

The Golden Turd (金のうんこ)

OK, so this is not the official name, but the Asahi Beer HQ and hall does look like it has a golden poo on top. This odd resemblance was apparently due to the architects drinking a few too many beers in a meeting, and it's one of those must take photos of Tokyo. *Sumida River*

Free sample food

Matsuya (松屋浅草)

One of the poshest department stores in Tokyo has a large food court offering a good variety of free snacks, drinks and more to try out. Particularly well known for old-school Japanese confectionery. *10am-8pm • Connected to Tobu Asakusa station*

Kappabashi (合羽橋)

True oddball tourism here. Fascinating street for restaurant and cafe owners to buy specialist goods, almost anything you could want for your kitchen can be found here. Merchants first started selling goods here as far back as 1912, and the area now has more than 170 specialist shops. From plastic food to furniture to ovens to cutlery, Kappabashi is worth checking out for an hour or two. Plus, as this is an area for restaurant owners, the prices for items such as cutlery can be very cheap. The plastic food can often be cheaper in shops like Tokyu Hands in Shibuya or Shinjuku though. *Tawaramachi station on Ginza Line*

Walk it and save: Asakusa to Kappabashi

From Asakusa station (Tokyo Metro) exits 1,2,3 or Asakusa Culture and Tourism Center, head down Kaminarimon Street in the opposite direction of Sumida river. Take a left turn at the end of the road and walk down to Tawaramachi station. Take a right turn, then Kappabashi is four blocks down on the right.

Budget food

Budget restaurants on map

1) Matsuya (松屋) - rice bowls and curry. *Gyudon bowls from 290 yen • 24h*
2) Kappa Sushi (かっぱ寿司) - conveyor belt sushi. *Sushi from 108 yen • 11am-10:30pm*
3) Fuji Soba (富士そば) - soba, udon and curry. *Soba from 300 yen • 24h*
4) Hidakaya (日高屋) - ramen and dumplings. *Ramen from 390 yen • 24h*
5) Mos Burger (モス) - Japanese burgers. *Burgers from 220 yen • 7am-10pm*
6) Yoshinoya (吉野家) - gyudon and curry. *Bowls from 330 yen • 24h*

Local budget food

There are some basic soba, udon and set meal restaurants on Kaminarimon Street, as well as these highlights:
7) Arashi Ramen (らあめん花月嵐) -Inventive seasonal soups and toppings. *Ramen from 780 yen • 11am-2am • Kaminarimon Street*
8) Sushizanmai (すしざんまい) - Conveyor belt sushi, good for a cheap light meal. *Sushi plates from 108 yen • 24h • Kaminarimon Street*
9) Origin Dining (オリジンダイニング) – Japanese set meals. *Sets from 580 yen • 11am-11:30pm • Down narrow street on left at exit 2 on Kaminarimon Street*

Cheap supermarkets (スーパー)

Best option is the Seiyu supermarket in ROX shopping mall (24h). Oseki supermarket is closer to the station on Kaminarimon Street (9:30am-9pm).

Shopping

100 yen shops

Seria (セリア) - Inside the Tobu Asakusa station complex. *10am-8pm*
Daiso (ダイソー) - Inside the ROX shopping mall. *10am-8pm*

Pharmacy (ドラッグストア)

Matsukiyo Papasu (どらっぐぱぱす) has a shop two minutes from the station on Kaminarimon street (10am-10pm).

How to get there and away

Asakusa is on the Tokyo Metro Ginza Line, Toei Asakusa Line and the starting point for Tobu trains to Nikko. From Shinjuku station, take the Marunouchi Line to Akasaka-mitsuke, then the Ginza Line to Asakusa station (30 mins, 240 yen). From Tokyo station, take the Marunouchi Line to Ginza, then take the Ginza Line to Asakusa station (25 mins, 200 yen). *Recommended rail passes: Tokyo Subway Ticket, Tokyo Metro 24-hour Ticket*

Tourist information (観光案内所)

One of the best equipped and staffed in Tokyo, the Asakusa Culture and Tourism Center is just outside Asakusa (Tokyo Metro) station exit 2 (9am-8pm).

Akihabara (秋葉原)

Akiba, as they call it here, is a geek's heaven. We are not sure how an area could be more perfect for geeks, from the cosplay girls hanging out on the streets, to the themed restaurants. Anything a geek, or otaku as they say here, needs is available here. For other people, Akihabara is a fascinatingly crazy place with lots of surprises. Shopping and geek experiences are the things to do here. The electronic shops may be cheaper or have slightly later versions of electronic, manga and anime items that you want. Many of the shops have English-speaking staff and goods that can be used abroad. As ever, tax-free options are everywhere.

Walk it and save!

Follow our recommended route on the map, and you will find all the arcades, maid cafes, manga and anime stores, electronic stores and used good stores that you need. Start from either side of the station. Take your time and enjoy the madness!

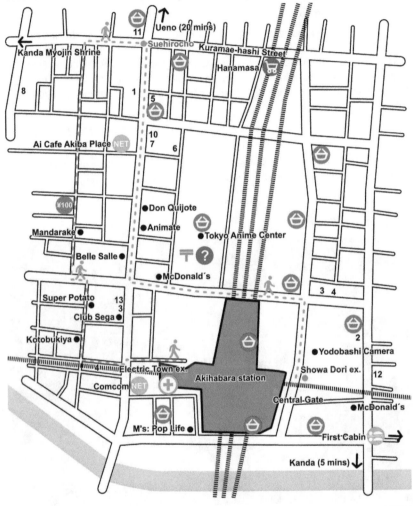

Things to do

Yodobashi Camera (ヨドバシカメラ)

Possibly the largest electronics shop in Tokyo, a good start to window shopping and people watching in Akihabara. Good choice of products aimed at foreign tourists, but you can often find better prices if you head to the other side of the station, to the electronic shops there. *9:30am-10pm • Outside JR Akihabara station Showa Dori exit*

Maids and Maid Cafes (メイドカフェ)

Akihabara is littered with many kinds of maid or cosplay cafes. The best way to see which one is for you, and get any latest deals or discounts, is to walk around the main streets on the map and ask the countless maids what's on offer. They may not speak much English, but will try hard to explain the basics. Ask about the "kabaa chaaji" (cover charge), as this is what often makes the cafes pricey (from around 1000 yen). If they are too pricey for you, you can just walk around and see the cute maids outside.

Chuo Dori

Don Quijote (ドン・キホーテ)

This branch has all the crazy items you would expect to be packed into a Don Quijote, from cheap green tea to cosplay clothes, but also has a large selection of otaku goods. Also has a maid cafe and game arcade. *9am-5pm • Chuo Dori*

Animate (アニメイト)

Another essential for any otaku shopping needs, just be sure to explore all the backstreets and Chuo Dori if you want to get the best price on something expensive. Animate has a large choice of manga, otaku videos and related merchandise. *10am-9pm • Chuo Dori*

Belle Salle Event Space (ベルサール)

Make sure you check out this event space when you are in Akihabara, as there are often free events for the general public. As this is Akiba, they tend to be related to gaming, anime, manga or geek fashion. Ask at the tourist information center for what's on. *Opening times according to event • Up Chuo Dori, just past Club Sega*

Club Sega (クラブ セガ)

One of the many game arcades in Akiba, with a good number of games remaining at 100 yen per play. Also has Purikura, photo booths where guests can have fun customizing and spicing up their pictures. *10am-11:30pm • Large red building on Chuo Dori*

Backstreets

Tokyo Anime Center (東京アニメセンター)

Another great spot for events and special exhibitions, but the shops tend to be a little pricier than others in the district. *11am-7pm • In the UDX building, the large complex to the north of JR Akihabara Electric Town exit (to the north west of station)*

Mandarake Complex

Anyone with a nerdy bone in their body will freak out at the awesomeness of this grand complex. Great selection of comics, figures and video games, plus some oddities you would expect from the otaku capital of the world. *12pm-8pm • Head up Chuo Dori, then head left just before Mister Donut and walk two blocks*

Super Potato

A treasure trove of retro gaming and gaming memorabilia. Try out a Virtual Boy, play old school games for a hundred yen in the arcade and check out the retro consoles and games. *11pm-8pm • Behind Club Sega on Chuo Dori*

Kotobukiya (コトブキヤ)

Another great mega store for buying all sorts of Otaku goods, or a perfect bit of window shopping in Akiba. The figurines are of particular interest here. Also has otaku souvenirs, such as character based chocolates and stationery. *10am-8pm • Opposite Super Potato*

M's: Pop Life (大人のデパート エムズ)

Have some fun walking around this high-rise adult store, with items you would never have imagined existed! *10am-11pm • Down street to left of JR Akihabara Electric Town exit*

Kanda Myojin Shrine (神田明神)

A major Shinto shrine near Akihabara and Ueno. More than 1000 years old, the buildings have been stunningly restored and the garden even more so. Japanese visit the shrine to pray, believing that worshipping here will give them luck in family life, business and will even help to find them a partner for marriage. As it's near Akiba, it has also become a kind of guardian for computer data as well, with luck charms on sale for "Protection and Safe keeper of I.T Data". *FREE • 24h • Walk north up Chuo Dori (Akiba's main street) and take the main road left when you get to Suehirocho station. You will see the shrine on the second block after the 7-Eleven convenience store*

100 yen shops

Can Do (キャンドゥ) - Near to Mandarake. *10am-9pm*

Budget food

Budget restaurants on map

1) Mos Burger (モス) - Japanese burgers. *Burgers from 220 yen • 7am-11pm*
2) Matsuya (松屋) - rice bowls and curry. *Gyudon bowls from 290 yen • 24h*
3) Yoshinoya (吉野家) - gyudon and curry. *Bowls from 330 yen • 24h*
4) Katsuya (かつや) - meat cutlet rice bowls. *Bowls from 490 yen • 7am - 11pm*
5) Hidakaya (日高屋) - ramen and dumplings. *Ramen from 390 yen • 24h*
6) Sukiya (すき家) - gyudon and curry. *Bowls from 360 yen • 24h*
7) Tenya (天丼てんや) - tempura. *Bowls from 500 yen • 11am-11pm*
8) Hotto Motto (ほっともっと) - bento boxes. *Bentos from 390 yen • 9am-9pm*

Local budget food

10) Mitsuya Soba (小諸そば) - Cheap soba and udon joint, with plastic food outside, so it's easy to choose your bowl. *Soba from 300 yen • Two blocks past Don Quijote on Chou Dori*
11) Taiyaki Kanda Daruma (たいやき神田達磨) - Classic taiyaki (fish-shaped sponge cake with custard or bean filling). *Taiyaki from 250 yen • Just outside Suehirocho station*
12) Coco Ichiban Curry House (カレーハウス CoCo 壱番屋) - The true taste of Japanese curry. *Curry + rice from 500 yen • 24h • Just outside Metro Hibiya exit 1/JR Akihabara Showa Dori exit*

13) Go!Go!CURRY (ゴーゴーカレー) - Darker and richer curry sauce, with some splendidly unhealthy toppings available! *Curry + rice from 530 yen • 10:55am-9:55pm • Next to Club Sega on Chuo Dori*

Cheap supermarkets (スーパー)

Hanamasa (肉のハナマサ) is a dirt cheap supermarket (24h). A little north of Akihabara station, to east of Suehirocho station, along Kuramae-Hashi Dori and under the train tracks.

Pharmacy (ドラッグストア)

Kokumin has a store in Atre Shopping Mall (アトレ), connected to JR Akihabara station on the west side, near the Electric Town exit (10am - 9pm).

How to get there and away

From Shinjuku station, take the Sobu Line to Akihabara station (18 mins, 160 yen). From Tokyo station, take the Yamanote line to Akihabara station (4 mins, 130 yen). It's also accessible via the Metro **Hibiya Line.** *Recommended rail passes: Tokyo Subway Ticket, Tokyo Metro 24-hour Ticket, Tokyo Metropolitan District Pass*

Tourist information (観光案内所)

In the UDX building (11am-5:30 pm, closed on Monday, Thursday).

Ryogoku (両国)

Ryogoku is a great choice for budget travelers, with a few free tourist sites that could easily take up a day. Home to the sumo tournaments in Tokyo, the area has the traditional atmosphere of old Tokyo. If you are only going to visit one or two museums in Japan, come to Ryogoku.

Sumo fighters preparing for battle!

Things to do

Edo-Tokyo Museum

A massive museum about the history of Tokyo, and its predecessor Edo. Features replicas and originals from as far back as the Edo era (between 1603 and 1868), a detailed timeline of the city and art from different periods. It will definitely take up at least half a day to see it all, so it's great value for money. Excellent English descriptions available. *Adults 600 yen, children and seniors 300 yen (FREE with Grutto Pass) • 9:30am-5:30pm (Saturday until 7:30pm). Closed Mondays • Just outside Ryogoku station •* http://www.edo-tokyo-museum.or.jp/en/

Sumo Museum (相撲博物館)

Created to show off the rich heritage of sumo in Ryogoku, and in Japan, and to preserve this for future fans of Japan's national sport. The museum has a host of displays showing the history of sumo, such as ceremonial aprons worn by various fighters and official rankings over the years. *FREE • 10am-4:30pm (closed Saturdays, Sundays, National Holidays) • Just outside Ryogoku station •* http://www.sumo.or.jp/En

Watch Sumo

A truly awesome experience, watching sumo really blew our socks off! Even if you don't speak Japanese, watching the fights and the ceremony around them in this all-day show will be one of your most culturally rewarding experiences in Japan. The grand, purpose-built stadium has enough traditional elements to keep the experience authentic, but all the modern facilities and takeaway joints a budget traveler needs. Just book as early as possible, otherwise prices can go sky high! *Tickets from 3800 yen (book and check schedule at* http://www.sumo.or.jp/EnTicket*) • January, May, September (two dates in each month)*

Former Yasuda Garden (旧安田庭園)

A medium sized traditional Japanese garden with great views of the SkyTree, and one of the prettiest free ones around. Built during the Genroku period (1688 - 1703), it feels like a miniature version of more famous Japanese gardens. The garden is also a nice place to check out during the cherry blossoms or autumn colors seasons. *FREE • 9am-4:30pm • Just behind the Sumo Museum, towards Sumida river*

Yokoamicho Park (横網町公園)

We were a little bit surprised to come across this peaceful park nearby, with its huge greenish pagoda-like temple. Also features memorials and gardens dedicated to those lost in earthquakes, Japan's constant menace. *FREE • 24h • Opposite back entrance/exit of Former Yasuda Garden*

Volunteer guides and tours

Edo-Tokyo Museum Volunteer Guides

Free tours of the permanent exhibition, which take about two hours. Head to the 6th floor Voluntary Guide Desk or a ticket counter to see if you can join a group. Two weeks' notice is advised, but if you can't do this, there is no harm in asking!

Travel discounts and packages

The Grutto Pass can be used to get free access to the Edo-Tokyo Museum, as well as to receive 20% off special exhibits.

Budget food

The best street to head for cheap food is the one on the south side of Ryogoku station. Here are some highlights, from west to east:

Saint Marc (サンマルクカフェ) - not super cheap, but sells reasonably priced croissants and coffee. Also has a free water fountain. *Croissants from 120 yen • 7am-11pm*

Saizeriya (サイゼリヤ) - light Italian dishes, such as a small pizza or pasta dish, this is a good spot. *Pizzas from 390 yen, pasta from 399 yen • 10am-12am*

Matsuya (松屋) - gyudon and burgers. *Meals from 290 yen • 24h*

Hidakaya Ramen (日高屋) - cheap ramen chain. *Ramen from 390 yen • 24h*

Kojiro Ramen (ラーメン餃子館 小次郎) - a more down to earth, old school gyoza dumplings and ramen joint. *Ramen from 580 yen • 11am-4am*

Hinoya Curry (日乃屋カレー) - Old school Japanese curry restaurant, with decently sized portions. *Curry rice from 730 yen • 11am-10pm*

Cheap supermarkets (スーパー)

There is a reasonably priced Maruetsu Petit (マルエツ プチ) supermarket (24h). Go to the Oedo Line station, and head out exit A5, then walk down in the opposite direction of the overhead tracks and to the left at the main road. It's across the road two blocks down.

Free wifi locations

There are plans to add wifi to the stations, but if they do not have it set up yet, head to Saint Marc cafe (サンマルクカフェ), opposite the south west side of the station.

How to get there and away

From Shinjuku station, take the Sobu Line to Ryogoku station (16 mins, 216 yen). From Tokyo station, take the Yamanote Line to Akihabara station, then the Sobu Line to Ryogoku station (9 mins, 154 yen). *Recommended rail pass: Tokyo Metropolitan District Pass, Tokyo Subway Ticket*

Tourist information (観光案内所)

Inside Ryogoku station (west side), open 10am-6pm.

Odaiba (お台場)

Set to be the main site of the 2020 Olympic Village, Odaiba is heading for some big changes. This man-made island was built during the boom economy in the 1980s, but when the bubble burst it was left to become a bit of a ghost town. The city has since opened up Odaiba to entertainments and shopping complexes, and the main area has been reborn as Tokyo's favorite date spot. Companies such as Fuji TV, with its futuristic HQ, and others have slowly moved into the area, creating an often vibrant waterfront. In the summer, come on the weekends as there are often free events or festivals on. Ask at a tourist information center for what's on.

Things to do

Odaiba Seaside Park (お台場海浜公園)

A nice place to take a stroll, with views of Tokyo city to the north. Come at night to take photos of the small Statue of Liberty (展望広場) replica, or chill out on the artificial beach in the daytime. *FREE • 24h • North of Odaiba-kaihinkoen and Tokyo Teleport stations*

Gundam Statue (ガンダム)

Mega statue of a Gundam robot, similar to Transformers in the west. Steam rushes out of the beast's vents in the evening. Immensely awesome! Was taken down in March 2017, projected to return autumn 2017. *FREE • 24h • Outside Diver City Tokyo Plaza*

Oedo-Onsen Monogatari Hot Spring (大江戸温泉物語)

Oedo Onsen Monogatari is an amazing hot spring, with various types of baths (including some lukewarm ones for beginners), Japanese restaurants and other lighthearted attractions. It's almost like a hot spring theme park. Included in the price is the rental of Yukatas (traditional Japanese robes), so visitors can walk around an Edo (old Tokyo) themed town! The Japanese section of its website often has discount coupons, so ask someone who can read Japanese to check before if you can't. *Adults 2612 yen (Sat & Sun 2828 yen) (500 yen discount after 6pm), children 1058 yen • 11am-9am • On south side, next to Telecom Center station*

Panasonic Center (パナソニックセンター)

This free exhibition shows off Panasonic's latest technology and prototypes for the future, including a 'home of the future' and a Nintendo showcase (2F). Not essential, but worth a visit if you have time. *FREE • 10am-5pm • Near Kokusai-Tenjijo station. Walk over Yumenoo Bridge (夢の大橋) and straight down 10 minutes*

Miraikan Museum of Emerging Science and Innovation (日本科学未来館)

A more in-depth technology showcase, this is the place to interact with the latest robots from companies such as Honda or Sony, with creations such as Asimo making appearances in the past. The museum has all the latest emerging technology from this tech-crazy country, with excellent English explanations provided in the vast exhibitions. *Adults 620 yen, children 210 yen • 10am-5pm (closed on Tuesday and New Year holidays) • Just north of Telecom Center station*

Toyota City Showcase (トヨタ シティ ショウケース)

Test drive the latest Toyota models and learn about the latest in automotive technology. The History Garage has more than 60 cars from across the generations, plus children can learn traffic rules while having a drive of their own 'petit cars'. *FREE • 11am-9pm • Inside Palette Town*

Shopping malls

Tokyo Teleport station in Odaiba is surrounded by several large shopping malls, all of which are great for window shopping or photo taking, but don't generally have any great deals or discounts compared to places such as Harajuku or Shinjuku. These are the best for budget travelers:

Palette Town (パレットタウン)

Huge complex, with a variety of themed zones and a Ferris wheel as well. Definitely check out Venus Port, which is a rather strange shopping center, supposed to look like some kind of grand Italian city, but all inside for convenience of course. *11am-9pm • Outside Aomi station*

Decks Tokyo Beach (デックス東京ビーチ)

Street performers show off their skills for free at the decking area outside this shopping mall. Inside is the rather expensive Sega Joypolis indoor theme park, but Daiba 1-chome Shoutengai on the second floor is full of fascinating knickknacks, retro souvenirs and cheap retro games to play. Top spot for odd souvenirs to take home. *11am-9pm • Between Tokyo Teleport station and Odaiba Seaside Park*

Diver City Tokyo Plaza (ダイバーシティ東京 プラザ)

Another large complex, the highlight (if it's around when you are there) being the above-mentioned Gundam statue outside. Apart from that, there are a host of chain stores including a branch of budget clothes manufacturer Uniqlo. *10am-9pm • Few mins west of Tokyo Teleport station*

100 yen shops

Seria (セリア) - Inside Venus Port in Palette Town. *11am-9pm*
Daiso (ダイソー) - Inside Diver City. *10am-9pm*

Pharmacy (ドラッグストア)

Decks Tokyo Beach has a Matsumotokiyoshi pharmacy (マツモトキヨシ) (10am - 9pm)

Budget food

It's generally a very touristy area, so prices tend to be high. There are some fun themed areas to enjoy, though.

Tokyo Ramen Stadium (東京ラーメン国技館 舞)

Stuff yourself with all kinds of ramen, from soy sauce to pork to full-on chili red ramen. Six of the best ramen chefs in the country have come together to create this very tasty experience. *Ramen from 980 yen • 11am-11pm • Aquacity (next to Decks Tokyo Beach) 5F*

Takoyaki Museum

If you are a fan of takoyaki (octopus balls), then this is the place for you. Features some much loved stalls from Osaka selling their local variants, plus shops to buy kits to make them yourselves. *Takoyaki from around 600 yen • 10am-9pm • Diver City Tokyo Plaza*

Cheap supermarkets (スーパー)

Although there are numerous convenience stores around, Maruetsu (マルエツ) has a larger range at its supermarket outside Odaiba-kaihinkoen station (9am - 10pm).

Water bottle refill spots

There is free Japanese tea and water in Oedo-Onsen Monogatari, but not many water fountains around. This may change as improvements are made for the 2020 Olympics.

How to get there and away

By free shuttle bus (大江戸温泉物語へのシャトルバス)

If you are going to Oedo Hot Spring, there is a free shuttle bus.

From Tokyo station
Leave from the Yaesu Central exit, cross the road and walk straight ahead 100 meters. The bus stop is in front of the 7-Eleven convenience store. *At 10:20, 12:50, 16:00, 17:50, 19:50.*

From Shinagawa
Leave from the Konan exit, head through Atre shopping mall and down to the main street heading out from the station on the left (behind the police box, with the Family Mart). Walk up, passing Sukiya (すき家 - show this character to someone if lost!) on the right side. At the first intersection turn left and walk down, then turn right. The shuttle uses bus stop No.1 by the Sony building. *Weekdays: 10:40, 13:20, 14:55, 17:35, 19:10, 20:25, 21:50. Weekends/Holidays: 10:10, 11:10, 12:10, 14:10, 15:10, 16:35, 17:35, 18:40, 20:10, 21:20, 22:40.*

By rail

From Shinjuku station, take the Saikyo Line to Osaki station, then the **Rinkai Line** to Tokyo Teleport (24 mins, 480 yen). Some Saikyo Line trains continue from Osaki on the **Rinkai Line**, so there is no need to change. From Tokyo station, take the Keiyo Line to Shin-Kiba station, then the **Rinkai Line** to Tokyo Teleport (22 mins, 420 yen).

Tourist information (観光案内所)

Just outside the Tokyo Teleport station gates is 'Odaiba Sky tourist information' (10am - 6pm).

Mount Takao (高尾山)

Autumn colors in Mount Takao

The cheapest and easiest to access mountain and hiking experience near Tokyo city. It really is a great deal, as the one hour train ride costs just 380 yen. There are various trails to take, depending on how much time you want to spend and how much you like to hike. There is also a cable car if you want to cut the journey time to the top in half. Along the way there are plenty of wonderful shrines, parks and nature to keep anyone interested. Casual hikers can take a cable car (8am-5:15pm, adults 480, children 240 yen), while those wanting more of a challenge should skip it and walk up trail #6 (entrance just to the left of the lower cable car station) *Difficulty: Easy to intermediate • Time required: 3-4 hours (take off about one hour if using the cable car)*

Keio Takaosan Onsen Gokurakuyu (京王高尾山温泉 極楽湯)

This brand new hot spring is a great spot to soak your feet and body in after a day of hiking. Includes a sauna and outdoor bath. *1000 yen • 8am-11pm • Behind Takaosanguchi station*

Discount pass: Mt. Takao Discount Ticket

Worth buying if you are sure you will need the cable car at Mount Takao. This ticket includes a return ticket from Shinjuku, plus a return or one-way ticket on the cable car. A 20% saving is given compared to buying separately. Buy at any Keio Line station in Tokyo city, such as in Shinjuku station.

Budget food

Keio Takaosan Onsen Gokurakuyu

There is also a Japanese restaurant inside the new hot spring, with a wide choice for all tastes. Curry, soba, sushi, it's got it all. *Meals from 750 yen • 8am-11pm (last order 10pm) • Behind Takaosanguchi station*

Mt. Takao Beer Mount

Beer garden 500 meters up Mount Takao with a commanding view of the mountains, it has to be one of the best in Tokyo and Kanto. Cheap buffet food available, with simple dishes like fried rice, dumplings and pasta. *Drinks from 600 yen, food from 1000-2000 yen • Weekdays 3pm-9pm, Weekends and holidays 2:30pm-9pm • Near cable car upper station*

Water bottle refill spots

There are no water refill spots going up the mountain and the vending machines are a little pricey near the start, so bring plenty of water with you.

Free wifi locations

Keio has free wifi available on the platform of Takaosanguchi station and at Keio Takaosan Onsen Gokurakuyu.

Recommended cheap accommodation

Hikage-sawa Campground (日影沢キャンプ場)

Basic campground, with a simple toilet and just 12 car parking spots. There are no rental facilities. If you can't speak Japanese, get someone at a previous hotel/hostel to call the campsite and check availability beforehand. *FREE • Irregular reception opening times • From Takaosanguchi station, take a Shō futsu (小仏行き) bound bus to Hikage (日影). Show the bus driver to be sure, as well as checking bus times when you arrive as services can be infrequent. You can also hike there in one hour from the summit • 042-663-6689*

How to get there and away

From Shinjuku station, take the Keio Line to Takaosanguchi station (370 yen, 1 hour). You may need to change at Kitano station. The way from Takaosanguchi station is well signposted.

Todoroki Valley (等々力渓谷)

Todoroki Valley is a wonderful retreat from all the hustle and bustle of Tokyo. Not far from Shibuya, it offers lush forests and luminously blue waters along a short 1.2 kilometer valley. Along the way there are a few small shrines and the odd waterfall, and the whole route is almost flat, so suitable for all ages. Puzzling why this place isn't on more tourist maps!

From Todoroki station, take the south exit, then walk to the right. Take a left turn down the main road and walk a little until you get to Seijo Ishii supermarket. The valley entrance is to the right of the supermarket. Walk down in a southerly direction, then when you get to the end return along the same route back to the station. *Difficulty: Easy • Walk time: 1 hour*

Budget food

There are a few cheap joints down the main shopping street. After heading out of Todoroki station (south exit) and walking to the right, take a right at the main road and walk over the tracks:

Sukiya (すき家) - curry and gyudon eat-in and takeaway. *Meals from 360 yen • 24h*
Origin Bento (オリジン弁当) - popular bento chain. *Bento boxes from 390 yen • 24h*
Hotto Motto (ほっともっと) - another good bento spot, with a more varied menu than Origin. *Bento boxes from 390 yen • 7am - 11pm*

Cheap supermarkets (スーパー)

There are plenty of convenience stores around the station, in addition to the Seijo Ishii supermarket (10am-11pm) on the walk. Seijo Ishii is not the cheapest of supermarkets, but has bakery bundles and some foreign food if you are missing something back home. A cheaper option is Super Value (スーパーバリュー), which is on the street to the left after passing the above mentioned Sukiya (10am-9pm).

Free wifi locations

Currently no stable free wifi around station or near valley. Return to Shibuya if you are desperate.

How to get there and away

From Shibuya station, take the Tokyu Toyoko Line to Jiyugaoka station. From here take the Tokyu Oimachi Line to Todoroki station (16 minutes, 200 yen).

Sugamo (巣鴨)

Amusingly known to Tokyoites as 'Harajuku for old ladies', Sugamo is a small area in Tokyo and a popular spot for domestic tourists to visit. Elderly Japanese people love to visit to buy items colored red, which they believe will bring them luck and good health in their older age. For foreign tourists, it's a highly recommended, quirky spot if you want to see what a tourist spot is like in Japan before it's full of tourist buses and tour groups! Prices are also more reasonable than the big tourist spots in Tokyo such as Harajuku, Odaiba and Shibuya.

Things to do

Jizo Dori Shopping Street

800 meter long street, this hotspot for old ladies has plenty of bargains (old Japanese ladies love to spend the whole day looking for a good deal!) and some people like to joke that, just like the look of the area, the prices are from the 1950s as well. While not as geared up for foreign tourists as other tourist streets, this is generally a friendlier and more laid-back area. As the main market here is for the elderly, many things are rather old fashioned and not affected by modernity. Not many chains here, just family-owned, traditional businesses and the occasional free sample of matcha tea or bean cake. *From JR Sugamo station's north exit or Metro exit A3, head north (opposite way to train bridge), Jizo Dori is the street on the left with the large gate, before the footbridge*

Rikugien Garden (六義園)

One of our favorite Japanese gardens in Tokyo. It's got it all; cherry blossoms, autumn colors, a reasonably priced tea house, a stunning lake and lots of interesting paths to take. Come in the evening during cherry blossoms and autumn color seasons for the 'light up' events. *Adults 300 yen, children free • 9am-5pm (closed Dec 29 - Jan 1) • Outside Komagome station*

Sakura Onsen (サクラ 東京染井温泉)

A modern hot spring in Tokyo that uses real hot spring water, a great place for your first hot spring experience in Japan. It also includes a traditional restaurant, where you can sit on Japanese tatami mats, a relaxation zone to chill out and massage services. Plus, you can get a haircut if you really want to! Save some money by bringing your own modesty towel and bath towel. *Adults 1296 yen, children 756 yen • 10am-11pm • By bus: Free shuttle bus every 10-15 minutes from Sugamo station (pink bus, stops near the JR south exit) or car park of swimming pool next to Sakura. On foot: up main road from the north exit, take a right just before the footbridge and walk down 5-10 minutes*

Kyu-Furukawa Gardens (旧古河庭園)

Could be described as a half English, half Japanese garden, so worth a visit if you have already been to plenty of traditional Japanese gardens. One half looks like a traditional English garden, with a manor house and roses, while the other half has a traditional Japanese pond and stone structures. Early May to early June is a great time to come for the roses and occasional free music events. *150 yen • 9am-5pm (closed Dec 29 - Jan 1) • From Komagome JR north exit or Metro exit 4, turn right (opposite side of bridge) and walk down the main road, staying on the left side. You will come to the entrance in 10 minutes*

Budget food

Jizo Dori Shopping Street

While best for cheap snacks and drinks, there are a few options for eat-in meals:

Oohashiya (地蔵そば 大橋屋) - Traditional soba and Japanese set meals. *Soba from 750 yen • 10am-6pm*
Sakurazen (桜膳) - Casual yakiniku (BBQ) and Korean food. Gets more expensive in the evening, so just come for the cheaper lunch sets. *Lunch from 800 yen • 11am-3pm, 5pm-11pm*

Outside Sugamo station (north exit)

Ootoya (大戸屋) - Various Japanese set meals. *Meals from 750 yen • 11am-2am*
Hidakaya Ramen (日高屋) - Tokyo's super cheap ramen chain. Fried rice and gyoza dumplings also available. *Ramen from 390 yen • 24h*
Matsuya (松屋) - Gyudon and burger eat-in and takeaway. *Meals from 290 yen • 24h*

Cheap supermarkets (スーパー)

There is a large Seiyu Supermarket (西友) near the JR north exit (24h), down the street to the left of the Jonathan's family restaurant.

Water bottle refill spots

Sakura Onsen has a water fountain in the changing rooms, so be sure to refill there.

Shopping

Apart from Jizo Dori, there are some shops on the way there, including a few 100 yen shops:
Can Do (キャンドゥイ) - Head to the right from JR Sugamo station, south exit. *10am-9pm*
Silk (シルク) - Another awesome 100 yen shop, just before you enter Jizo Dori shopping street. *10am-9:30pm*

Getting around

It takes only 15 minutes or so to walk from Sugamo station to Komagome station or vice versa, to save on the train ticket. Just use a map in the station to make sure you are going in the right direction and head down the track. The tourist hotspots are short walks from either station, so the Sugamo area is a great way to spend an afternoon.

How to get there and away

From Shinjuku station, take the Yamanote Line to Sugamo station (16 mins, 170 yen). From Tokyo station, take the Yamanote Line to Sugamo station (18 mins, 170 yen). Komagome is the next station on the line. By Tokyo Metro, take the Namboku Line to Sugamo station. *Recommended rail passes: Tokyo Subway Ticket, Tokyo Metro 24-hour Ticket, Tokyo Metropolitan District Pass*

Kanto region: around Tokyo

Tokyo is situated in Kanto, the most built up and prosperous of all the prefectures in Japan. The prefecture has a great transportation network, with many spots not far away, making Tokyo a perfect base from which to do some side trips on a budget. The highlight is of course Mount Fuji, a great challenge that any traveler should tick off their bucket list. Other highlights include the relaxing hot spring town of Hakone, the spiritual temple town of Nikko and Tokyo's little brother city of Yokohama. The multiple discount transportation passes are perfect for budget travelers.

Discount pass: JR Tokyo Wide Pass

Most of the spots in this chapter have discount transportation passes of their own, but if you want to do many of them in a short amount of time, the JR Tokyo Wide Pass may be worth a look. It allows unlimited use of JR trains (and a few partner lines) in the Kanto prefecture for three consecutive days, including use of Shinkansen and limited express trains. The pass is available from a JR Travel Service Center in any major station in Tokyo or Yokoyama, plus Narita and Haneda airports. Note the pass is for those with visitor visas only.

The JR Tokyo Wide Pass covers most of the places in this chapter. It provides access to Kamakura, Kawagoe, Nikko, Omiya and Bonsai Village and Yokohama. It would be possible to visit one of these each day, so have a look and see which take your fancy. The pass does not include the unlimited use of local transportation in these areas, which the individual passes for tourist areas do. The following spots require a short journey on a train line or bus not covered by the pass: Hakone (310 yen extra from Odawara station) and Mount Fuji (2100 yen extra from Kawaguchiko station). In conclusion, if you are in a rush and want to really pack in lots in those three days, this pass is worth it, but otherwise it's probably easier and cheaper to get each area's own discount pass, or individual cheap local or express train tickets. *Adults 10000 yen, children 500 yen*

Yokohama (横浜)

Actually the second largest city in Japan and only 30 minutes from Tokyo, Yokohama has long since become part of the grand metropolis. What sets this city apart is its port and the rich history of foreign culture and trade. Makes for a fun day trip, especially if you have already done lots of Tokyo before. When you arrive, head to the nearest tourist information center and pick up one of their large maps. If you are using the **Minato Mirai Line**, our recommended spots are shown, but it also features seasonal walking routes.

Discount pass: Minato Mirai Line One Day Pass

The best way to get to and around Yokohama. Minato Mirai Line One Day Pass allows visitors to use the **Minato Mirai Line** an unlimited amount of times in Yokohama, plus use of a return ticket from Shibuya in Tokyo on the Tokyu Line if required. If you don't want to walk around all day (distances can be large here) and want to save time by using the trains, this is a great pass. If you really love walking a lot, you could just walk around Yokohama with a map from the tourist information center in the station. Buy it from the Tokyu ticket offices. *From Tokyo: Adults 840 yen, Children 420 yen. From Yokohama station: Adults 460 yen, Children 230 yen*

A little bit of history

Way back in 1859, Yokohama was a small village of 600 when it opened its first port. The city from then on started to blossom as a modern trading post, in particular in the export of Japanese tea and silk. The Great Kanto Earthquake destroyed much of Yokohama in 1923, but it was not long before the city returned to its former glory. Devastation to the city came again in World War Two and the city was initially slow to redevelop. Thankfully Japan's economic boom came along in the 80s and 90s, triggering rapid growth and leading to a very modern, clean city.

Things to do

Minato Mirai 21 District

The following are all near Minato Mirai station on the **Minato Mirai Line**:

Cupnoodles Museum (カップヌードルミュージアム)

A strange but wonderful museum. From the first chicken noodles, to the hundreds of current variations, this museum is all about instant noodles and their inventor, Momofuku Ando. There is also a world noodle food court, strange noodle-based art and a noodle kitchen to make your own custom noodles. A real 'only in Japan' experience, and fun for all the family. *Adults 500 yen, Children FREE • 10am-6pm (closed New Year holidays and Tuesdays. When Tuesday is a holiday, closed the following day)*

Yokohama Cosmo World (コスモワールド)

Much cheaper, and more nostalgic, than going to Disney World. Visitors can buy individual ride tickets to keep costs down at this compact theme park, with a water ride, roller coaster, Ferris wheel and game arcades. *FREE entry (rides 300-700 yen) • Weekdays 11am-9pm, weekends 11am-10pm (closed Thursdays)*

Yokohama Red Brick Warehouses (横浜赤レンガ倉庫)

Back in the 1920s, these mega brick warehouses were the Customs Inspection House for boats coming into the harbor. It has since been converted into a hip area for families and tourists. Best for budget travelers are the frequent festivals, usually on weekends, such as October Beer Fest in autumn, ice skating in the winter and free concerts in the summer. *FREE • 10am-7pm*

Yokohama Museum of Art (横浜美術館)

A wide, but manageable collection of art. The main sections have late 19th century works from artists such as Milo, Picasso and Dali, while others feature artists with ties to Yokohama. Features excellent English explanations and children's workshops, plus occasionally has free access days. *Adults 500 yen, high school children and above 300 yen, elementary and under 100 yen • 10am-6pm (closed New Year holidays and Thursdays if not holiday)*

Yokohama Landmark Tower (ランドマークタワー)

Get a view 273 meters above Yokohama, after enjoying a 750 meters per minute elevator. Not essential, but most travelers head up on clear days as the tower also provides stunning views over to Tokyo. *Adults 1000 yen, children 200-800 yen • 10am-9pm*

Yamashita

Head to Nihon-Odori station on the **Minato Mirai Line** to visit Yokohama's famous port area:

Yamashita Park (山下公園)

Yokohama's main park and a good spot to start your adventures. In the summer there are usually events here every week.

Osanbashi Yokohama International Passenger Terminal (大さん橋)

Very funky design for this ultramodern passenger terminal. Made of strips of wood, the winding structure is very unique piece of abstract architecture. Well worth a relaxing stroll, especially with a beer at night, watching over the city lights.

Chinatown (中華街)

Japan's biggest Chinatown, dwarfing most others. As you walk around, there will be more than a few sellers offering free samples of Chinese snacks or drinks, but maybe not as many bargains as you may be expecting. Budget travelers should completely avoid going to the restaurants on the main street as they have a bad reputation for charging tourist prices, but some of the side streets can be more reasonable.

Motomachi (元町)

A nice area featuring lots of registered historical buildings, parks and churches. Feels like a mix between Japan and Europe. Some of the buildings charge a small fee for entrance, but there are plenty of free options, so no need to pay unless you are particularly into the history and architecture of Yokohama. There are more than a dozen such buildings and sites to see, but here are the best spots to check out:

Ehrisman Residence

Finished in 1926 as the residence of Fritz Ehrismann, a prominent exporter and importer of sought-after products like silk. His vast wealth allowed him to commission Antonin Raymond to design the building, who was considered to be a master of modern architecture at the time. *FREE • 9:30am-5pm (6pm in summer) (closed New Year holidays)*

Yokohama Foreign General Cemetery

Often closed, but have a look to see if it's open when you are there. Back when Commodore Perry came to Japan in 1854 with several warships to force the country to open up to trade, one of his marines perished. This cemetery was therefore formed as a burial ground for Americans, and other foreigners after this incident. *FREE • Noon-4pm (normally closed, but open on weekends and holidays Mar - Dec)*

Berrick Hall

The local residence of British trading merchant B.R. Berrick, this building was constructed in 1930. It later served as the dormitory for an international school, but since 2000 has been open to the general public. Once you get here, you will soon realize why it is such an in-demand wedding venue, with its picturesque grounds and classic interior. *FREE • 9:30am-5pm (6pm in summer) (closed New Year holidays)*

Bluff No. 234

Prettily lit up in the evening, this building dates back to 1927, when it was an apartment for the new foreigners entering via Yokohama Bay. Detailed panels help to enlighten guests about the history of the area. There are also some other free 'Bluffs' around the area. *FREE • 9:30am-5pm (6pm in summer) (closed New Year holidays)*

Shin-Yokohama Ramen Museum

We sure did stuff ourselves here. Calling itself a "ramen amusement park", this museum is a fantastic way to try various types of Japanese noodles. Portions can be small, but the usually lower prices should allow you to try out a few, including giving the crazier, and spicier, varieties a try. Nine ramen shops inside. *Adults 300 yen, children 100 yen, under 6 FREE • 11am-11pm • Just north of Shin-Yokohama station*

Volunteer guides and tours

Kanagawa Good Will Guide Club - http://www.ksgg.org/index.html
Offers a guided tour along Yokohama waterfront, so includes all the highlights. Try to book more than two weeks in advance.

Budget food

Yokohama is quite spread out, so if you do come across somewhere cheap, and it's around time to eat, grab the chance and head inside. Having said that, there is a high concentration of convenience stores here.

Yokohama World Porters

There are a few cheap spots in Yokohama World Porters shopping mall, opposite the Cup Noodle Museum in Minato Mirai:

Saizeriya (サイゼリヤ) - Light Italian dishes, such as a small pizza or pasta dish. *Pizzas from 390 yen, pasta from 399 yen • 10am-11pm*

Ofukuya Ramen (大ふく屋) - Classic ramen, lots of varieties to choose from. *Ramen from 780 yen • 11am-10:30pm*

Steak Mountain (鉄板ステーキチャーハン) - Steaks on fried rice. *Plates from 790 yen • 10:30am-9pm*

Landmark Tower

There is a large selection in Landmark Tower, as well as in the connected Queen's Square. Most are quite expensive, but there are a few good budget options:

Tsukemen Tetsu (つけめん TETSU) - Famous dipping noodles shop, with some super tasty soup. *Meals from 780 yen • 11am-11pm*

Vie De France (ヴィ・ド・フランス) - Reasonably cheap bakery and cafe, which often cuts prices in the evening. *Breads from 150 yen • 7:30am-9pm*

Soup Stock Tokyo (スープ ストック トーキョー) - Great if you need a light meal. Fresh new soups every day. *Sets from around 800 yen • 8am-10pm*

Cheap supermarkets (スーパー)

If you in Yokohama station, the best is Tokyu Store (東急ストア) on the north side of the building (10am-10pm). Near Chinatown, outside Motomachi-Chukagai station is Maruetsu Petit (マルエツ プチ), a large 24-hour supermarket (opposite exit 2). There are also numerous small supermarkets around.

Water bottle refill spots

Yamashita Koen has some water fountains, as does Motomachi Koen (元町公園) in the Motomachi area and the park on the coast in Minato Mirai.

Shopping

100 yen shops

Daiso (ダイソー) - Inside 'Mark Is' shopping mall (マークイズみなとみらい), next to Minato Mirai station (10am-8pm). There is also one outside Yokohama station, west exit, opposite Yodobashi Camera, plus on Chukagai Odori (main street in Chinatown).

Seria (セリア) - In World Portal (ワールドポーターズ), the shopping mall opposite Cosmo World in Minato Mirai. *10:30am-9pm*

Pharmacy (ドラッグストア)

Matsumoto (マツモトキヨシ) has a store inside Yokohama station (10am-10pm).

Recommended cheap accommodation

Hostels and guest houses

Hayashi Kaikan (Yokohama Hostel Village)
Probably the cheapest place to stay in Yokohama. Hardly the Ritz, but you can't argue with these prices! Not totally central, but a short walk from all the action. *Dorms from 2400 yen •* http://yokohama.hostelvillage.com/en/

Hostel Zen
Another well-known hostel, which is smaller than others and seems to have a nice, friendly atmosphere. Various plans and rooms types available. *Dorms from 2800 yen*

Capsule hotels and overnight spas

Sky Spa Yokohama
Quite a selection of baths they have here! Modern, centrally located and with clean capsules to sleep in. *Overnight passes from 4700 yen • In Marui City, to east side of Yokohama station*

Spa & Capsule Hotel Grand Park-Inn Yokohama
More of a standard capsule hotel than the others, so prices are a little lower, though there are some spa facilities. In a slightly seedy area, but not in any way too much so. *Capsules from 3500 yen • West side of Yokohama station, near subway exit 9. Walk to right, then take first right after a bit, then left and down*

Manyo Club (横浜みなとみらい 万葉倶楽部)
Super fun, or relaxing, way to spend your evening, night and morning. Large variety of baths, including outside ones overlooking Tokyo Bay, game arcades, stone relaxation rooms and more. Overnighters can catch 40 winks in the lazyboy chairs, or in the tatami rooms. *Overnight passes from 4500 yen •*
http://www.manyo.co.jp/mm21/eng/

Internet cafes (ネットカフェ)

The biggest collection of net cafes is on the west side of Yokohama station. It's fun to have a look around, but go to these safe bets if you are new to net cafes:

Manbo (マンボー)
Free showers, comics and drinks. They also have other branches nearby, so ask if they are full. *Five hours (5 時間パック) from 1250 yen, 480 yen for additional hours • Bit tricky to get to, so use wifi in Yokohama station. Near subway exit 9*

Hanatato (花太郎)
Some amazing deals, especially on weekdays. Showers included, plus the usual free drinks. You can leave and come back on night packages. *13 hours night package (ナイトパック) from 2100 yen • Also tricky to get to, so use wifi in Yokohama station. Near subway exit 9*

How to get there and away

If on the west wide of Tokyo, it's usually cheapest to go via Shibuya. From Shibuya station, take the Tokyu Toyoko Line to Yokohama station (30 mins, 200 yen or covered with the Minato Mirai Line One Day Pass). From Tokyo station on the east side of Tokyo, take the JR Tokaido Line to Yokohama station (30 mins, 470 yen).

Tourist information (観光案内所)

Inside Yokohama station's central passage (9am-7pm), Shin-Yokohama station for the Shinkansen (9am-9pm) and Sakuragicho station (9am-6pm).

Nikko (日光)

Toshogu Shrine, Nikko

Probably the most impressive side trip from Tokyo, Nikko is one of Japan's many UNESCO World Heritage sites. It's a town full of temples, shrines, waterfall and lakes. The World Heritage area includes two shrines and a temple, but there are lots of other cheap touristy things to do as well. There are also a few non-traditional, crazy experiences, such as the Edo inspired theme park and a miniatures theme park. Excellent English language signage and maps.

Discount passes: Tobu Nikko Passes

From Asakusa in Tokyo, Tobu Railways has three kinds of passes. They are an obvious pick for budget travelers, as there is not much else in the area apart from the locations on the passes, and everything can be comfortably done in the time allowed. You can buy them at the Tobu Sightseeing Service Center in Tobu Asakusa station. The passes include unlimited use of buses (and trains if applicable) to the main spots. Because some of the areas in Nikko are quite spaced out, you will need to use the bus at least a few times. You will almost certainly save money.

Discounts included

20% off limited express tickets (only saves 30 mins or so, so not essential), 5% off at some shops in Asakusa, 10% off for purchases over 1000 yen at some shops in Nikko and discounts to over a dozen tourist spots in Nikko. Look for the logos in the pass for where you can get money off.

Nikko City Area Pass

The 2 Day Nikko Pass is the best way to visit Nikko and Kinugawa Onsen for most budget travelers. The two days provide plenty of time to see all the main shrines and temples in this UNESCO World Heritage site area. It includes a round ticket from Tokyo. *Adults 2670 yen, children 1340 yen*

Nikko All Area Pass

4 days are included on this pass, as well as expanded use of the bus network beyond the main tourist spots, including to the onsen towns in the north. *April-November: Adults 4520 yen, children 2280 yen. December-March: Adults 4150 yen, children 2070 yen*

Theme Park and Nikko City Area Pass

Similar to the Nikko City Pass, but includes tickets to one or both of the main theme parks, and use of the bus route between them. *Tobu World Square + Edo Wonderland Nikko Edomura: Adults 8010 yen, children 4010 yen. Tobu World Square: 4710 yen, children 2360 yen. Edo Wonderland Nikko Edomura: Adults 6610 yen, children 3310 yen*

Things to do

Toshogu Shrine (日光東照宮)

The most well-known World Heritage shrine in Nikko, and recently renovated. It enshrines the first Shogun of the Edo Shogunate, Tokugawa Ieyasu. This temple complex leads into the forested mountain, and will blow you away with its stunning buildings and national treasures (8 national treasures and 34 important cultural properties in total). Head up the stone stairs at the back for a cool walk up to another shrine up the small mountain. *Adults 800, children 600 yen • 8am-5pm (8am-4pm in the winter) • 'Nishi-sando' bus stop*

Shinkyo Bridge (神橋)

Beautiful wooden Japanese red bridge, at the entrance to the Nikko mountains. The myth goes that when a head priest, named Shodo Shonin, was not able to cross the Daiyagawa River he was helped by the gods. Two snakes appeared and constructed the bridge so he could cross. *FREE • 'Shinkyo' bus stop, then follow signs. Walkable from nearby shrines*

Rinno-ji Temple (日光山輪王寺)

A large temple surrounded by huge trees, this is one of the largest wooden structures in the area. Founded more than 1000 years ago, the complex features a grand hall with statues of various gods, a treasure house exhibiting statues of Buddha and other important cultural properties. Also as a Japanese garden called Shoyoen. *Adults 1000 yen, children 600 yen • 8am-5pm (8am-4pm in the winter) • 'Nishi-sando' bus stop*

Futarasan Temple (二荒山神社)

A quiet temple within the forests of Nikko, and a site for followers to worship nearby Mount Futarasan. It's famous for offering good luck to those who pray in the forest-enclosed complex, for important life changes such as pregnancy or marriage. A soon as you arrive you will realize why Nikko is a World Heritage site. *200 yen • 8am-5pm (8am-4pm in the winter) • 'Nishi-sando' bus stop, or walk from Shinkyo bridge*

Taiyuin Temple (大猷院)

A big complex of temple buildings in the forested mountains, this is the mausoleum of Tokugawa Iemitsu. It was constructed to face Toshogu Shrine, but in a subtle way, so as to not overshadow it. The main hall and front shrines are registered as national treasures, but explore around as there are some excellent examples of ancient craftsmanship in the various structures. *550 yen • 8am-6pm • 'Nishi-sando' bus stop, or walk from Shinkyo bridge*

Kegon Waterfall (華厳の滝)

A tall waterfall not far from the center of Nikko, and the most popular. The water from Lake Chuzenji falls almost 100 meters, and the viewing platforms give a good view from below. Great any time of the year. *550 yen • 8am-5pm (9am-4:30pm in the winter) • 'Chuzenji-onsen' bus stop*

Lake Chuzenji (中禅寺湖)

Created more than 20,000 years ago when Mount Nantai erupted. This 11.62 km squared lake was once surrounded by foreign embassies and estates in the Meiji period, so was known for its beauty for many years before tourists arrived. Have a walk around the lake and take some great photos to take home. *FREE • 'Tachikikannon-iriguchi' bus stop or short walk from Kegon Waterfall*

Ryuzu Waterfall (竜頭ノ滝)

On the north-west of Lake Chuzenji is this nice waterfall and park, a quieter spot than Kegon Waterfall. If you have time, walk up to Lake Yunoko and Yudaki Falls. *FREE • 'Akanuma' bus stop*

Tobu World Square (東武ワールドスクウェア)

A lighthearted, and up-to-date outdoor museum with miniature reproductions of more than 100 famous buildings and structures from across the world. Appropriately for Nikko, it includes 45 World Heritage sites at a 1/25 scale. *2800 yen (see website to check for 500 yen discount coupon), FREE with Theme Park and Nikko City Area Pass • 8am-5pm (8am-4pm in the winter) • Get bus from Kinugawa-onsen station, near to Nikko •* https://www.tobuws.co.jp/en/

Edo Wonderland Nikko Edomura (日光江戸村)

Experience the old city of Edo (former name of Tokyo), at this faithful, but fun reproduction. The houses, downtown area and ninja village are great if you need a break away from all the temples. Also interesting to see the 'locals' walking around, doing their daily tasks and jobs. *One Day Pass: adults 4700 yen, children 2400 yen. Afternoon Pass (from 2pm, or 1pm in winter): adults 4100 yen, children 2100 yen (see website to check for 10% discount coupon), FREE with Theme Park and Nikko City Area Pass • 9am-5pm (9:30am-4pm in the winter) • Get bus from Kinugawa-onsen station, nearby Nikko •* http://edowonderland.net/en/

Hike for free

There are plenty of hikes that start from near the town center or are a short distance from a bus stop, but there are a few real highlights. More routes can be found in the tourist information centers, where free hiking and walking maps are available.

Mount Nakimushi

Famous mountain, which can be accessed just south of the train stations. Small waterfalls, pristine forest and the religious ornaments along the way make it an enjoyable hike. *Difficulty: Medium • Hike time: 4-5 hours*

Lake Chuzenji

A variety of routes are available, but the South-Bank Course (starting from near Kegon Waterfall) is a nice balance of lake and hills. *Difficulty: Easy • Hike time: 4-5 hours*

Lake Yunoko

This smaller lake is a perfect quick and easy hike, which offers views of Yudaki Falls and the nearby Onsen Shrine. Access from Yudaki Falls bus stop. *Difficulty: Easy • Hike time: 1 hour*

Volunteer guides and tours

Utsunomiya SGG Club - http://www016.upp.so-net.ne.jp/usgg/
Provides guides for Nikko from the nearby city of Utsunomiya. This does mean you have to pay for them to come to Nikko, but it's still a good deal if you want an in-depth experience. Apply at least two weeks in advance.

Budget food

Few budget chain restaurants in the area, presumably to keep the place more authentic. Head north up Nihon Romantic Highway from the Nikko station for a selection of restaurants, but they are quite spaced out. There are some classic tonkatsu (deep fried cutlet) and ramen joints up here, but good prices may be hard (and time consuming) to find. If you are stuck around the station, head to the supermarket for a large choice of cheap takeouts and microwavable items.

Cheap supermarkets (スーパー)

Lion Dor (リオン・ドール) is five-minute walk from Tobu Nikko station. Head out and then walk down the road with the post office on the right (9am-9pm). There are also a small number of convenience stores around.

Water bottle refill spots

Bring a large bottle of water from your hostel/hotel, just in case you can't or don't go to a restaurant with some way to refill.

Shopping

100 yen shops

meets (ミーツ) - Down the river to the north side of the station. *9am-9pm*

Pharmacy (ドラッグストア)

Welcia (ウエルシア) - From the JR Nikko station, head down the road to the left of Nikko Station Hotel Classic, then take a left at the second traffic lights and walk a few minutes. *9am-9pm*

Recommended cheap accommodation

Hostels and guest houses

Minsyuku Rindo-no-ie
Very cheap hostel with Japanese tatami floors and friendly customer service. Also has a large bath. *Dorms from 3500* • http://outdoor.geocities.jp/rindoutyan/

Nikko Suginamiki Youth Hostel
Great if you are a Youth Hostel member, this place is also good for small groups. *Dorms from 3360 yen* • http://www.jyh.or.jp/e/i.php?jyhno=2208

Nikko Guesthouse Sumica
Traditional rooms with Japanese tatami mats and a really friendly atmosphere. Right next to the station, yet still some of the cheapest rates. *Dorms from 2800* • http://nikko-guesthouse.com/en_index.html

Campsites

Nikko has a few campsites a short drive from the station, or a 15-minute walk in the case of Nikko Daiyagawa Park. None currently have English booking available, so ask someone at a tourist information center or prior accommodation to call, if you want to check availability before going. Prices are from around 2000 yen per tent site.
New Kirifuri Campsite (ニュー霧降キャンプ場) - 0288-53-4728 • http://www.kirifuri-camp.com/
Nikko Daiyagawa Park (日光だいや川公園オートキャンプ場) - 0288-23-0201 • https://www.park-tochigi.com/daiyagawa/
Manakanomori (まなかの森 キャンプ) - 0288-21-7748 • http://www.nikko-manakanomori.com/index.html

How to get there and away

From Asakusa station in Tokyo, take a **Tobu Line** Rapid train (2 hours) to Nikko. Free with the passes, or 2700 yen.

Tourist information (観光案内所)

In JR Nikko station (8am-5:30pm) and Tobu Nikko station (8:30-5pm), as well as 10 minutes up Nihon Romantic Highway from the stations (9am-5pm).

Mount Fuji (富士山)

Japan's most iconic mountain, now a UNESCO World Heritage site, should be on the top of most travelers' plans for a trip to the land of the rising sun. The highest mountain in Japan at 3,776 meters, its grand size straddles over various prefectures. It is also one of Japan's "Three Holy Mountains" and has been the site of pilgrimage to Japanese people for centuries. In Shinto mythology, the god Kuninotokotachi is believed to reside at the top. For us mere mortals, the view from the top of Mount Fuji has to be seen to be believed. While it can get very busy, this will probably be your most memorable experience in Japan and it's surprisingly cheap to visit. Just be sure to bring a warm coat for the chilly summit!

Yoshida Trail

Most budget travelers should take this, as getting there is cheapest. While it can be steep and challenging, even to the fairly fit, it's a great reward to get to the views at the top. *Difficulty: Medium • Hike time: 9-10 hours return • Hiking season: Around July 1 to Sept 1*

When to come

The best time to arrive is in the evening. If you start heading up by 9-10pm, by the time you get to the top you should have perfect timing to watch the spectacular sunrise. It's truly one of the most amazing sights you will ever see. Plus walking up overnight saves on having to book a room somewhere. Another tip is to come on the weekdays and outside holidays, to avoid large families with children.

Budget food

While there are some souvenir shops and restaurants around the bus stop, the prices are not so good and choice is limited for food to actually take up. Surprisingly, there are some noodle stalls up the mountain, but prices are really high and these stalls should be avoided unless you are starving. Go to a supermarket the night before and get yourself plenty of drinks and food for the long hike.

Water bottle refill spots

There are no free water fountains as you head up, and the price of drinks (yes, there is a vending machine at the top!) get very expensive, to the point that prices for drinks are about four times what they normally are at the shop on the summit.

Pharmacy (ドラッグ ストア)

The shops at the base have some basics, but bring any essential medicine.

Recommended cheap accommodation

There are several mountain huts on the way up, all of which charge to stay. Prices are rather high for a basic hut experience, but if you feel 8-10 hours walking all in one go is too much for you, they are worth it. Fujisan Mountain Guides can also provide a booking service in English (1000 yen), if you are having trouble finding a bed. Reservations are usually taken from April. These two have English websites, but try to reserve as soon as possible to hold your spot:

Kamaiwa-kan (鎌岩館)

Brand new, stylish building about halfway up, so a perfect spot to have a sleep before continuing up. Can also provide basic food like curry or burgers. *Bed from 5800 yen with no meals on weekdays, 8400 yen on weekends (with two meals)* • http://kamaiwakan.jpn.org/

Haku-un-so (白雲荘)

Very near to the summit, this hut will break your journey in half. With more than 300 beds, this place can get packed, but the prices are pretty good for the location. Food can also be provided, and there is a small shop if you have forgotten anything. *Bed from 5800 yen with no meals* • http://fujisan-hakuun.com/en/reservation/

How to get there and away

From Tokyo, the cheapest and fastest way is to get a highway bus from Shinjuku Bus Terminal in Shinjuku, with Keio Bus (operated May through October). You must reserve in advance at the terminal or on the Keio Bus website. The tickets cost 2700 yen (discounts may be given if you book more than a month ahead, children half price). From Kawaguchiko station in Fuji Five Lakes, Keio Bus also run regular services (2100 yen for round trip, children half price). You could use this bus if traveling on a JR Tokyo Wide Pass or national JR Rail Pass.

Tourist information (観光案内所)

Near the bus stop (May 1 - Oct 31, 9am-4:30pm, until 8pm July 1 - Sept 11).

Hakone (箱根)

Tokyo's most popular side trip. There is something for everyone here, from hiking to shopping to volcano viewing and hot springs. The town is part of Fuji Hakone Izu National Park, which offers stunning views of Mount Fuji. In addition to this there are lots of standout features such as Owakudani, an eerie volcanic area with lots of yellow fumes, Lake Ashi with its pirate sightseeing boat tour and the Hakone Tozan Train which heads up the mountain. What makes Hakone stand out for budget travelers is the Hakone Free Pass, which offers unlimited transportation in the area and loads of discounts. It really makes Hakone an easy place to get around. Maps and signs are all in English as well, so no chance of getting lost hiking!

Discount pass: Hakone Free Pass

The Hakone Free Pass from Odakyu Railway is the best and cheapest way to visit Hakone. It provides unlimited use of the cable car, ropeway, tourist boats, trains and buses in the area, plus the ride from Shinjuku station and back. It also provides discounts or free access to around 50 places in Hakone. Some things in Hakone, especially the ropeway, can get super expensive if you don't have the pass, so it's usually a must buy for budget travelers. You can buy it at the Odakyu Sightseeing Service Center in Shinjuku station or at ticket machines. *Two Day Pass: Adults 5140 yen, Children 1500 yen. Three Day Pass: Adults 5640 yen, Children 1750 yen.*

A little bit of history

At the start of the Edo period, Hakone became a post station on the Tokaido Highway connecting Edo (the old Tokyo) with Kyoto. It became an important checkpoint on the route, which visitors can see a recreation of at the Hakone Sekisho and Checkpoint. Under the strict Tokugawa Shogunate, everyone coming in or leaving was checked and their items inspected by officials. The aim was to restrict the travel of weapons and of women. After the Meiji Restoration, Hakone slowly grew into a fully-fledged town and the Imperial household established a summer villa here, close to the lake. Visitors can also visit this.

Things to do

Owakudani (大涌谷)
A must-see in Hakone, get off at Owakudani station on the ropeway and try some 'kuro-tamago' (black eggs). They have been boiled in the hot spring water, so have black shells! Watch the yellowy volcanic gases blow out of the ground and the fresh hot spring water spew out over the mountain. *FREE • 8:30am-5pm • Owakudani station on ropeway*

Hakone Shrine (箱根神社)
A stunning Shinto shrine complex, starting from a red gate standing in Lake Ashi, running up into the mountain. Apparently founded in 757, the original shrine was

said to reside at the summit of Mount Komagatake. It became important for samurai, who would come to pray for luck in their various endeavors. *FREE • 24h*

Hakone Detached Palace Garden (恩賜箱根公園)

The old Imperial family summer house and gardens are now free for you to roam around and take photos of. Walking up into the park gives visitors amazing views over the lake and of Mount Fuji. *FREE • 9am-4:30pm • Onshi-Koen-mae bus stop (route H)*

Hakone Sekisho and Checkpoint (箱根関所)

An authentic recreation of the old trading checkpoint and surrounding village. The people who built this utilized old carpentry and masonry techniques from the Edo period, to make sure everything looks as authentic as possible. *FREE • 9am-5pm • Hakone Sekisho-ato bus stop (route H)*

Sightseeing cruise on Lake Ashi (箱根海賊船)

A rather silly, but amusing way to get across the lake. This 18th century-style ship has been taken over by pirates, like a scene from Pirates of the Caribbean. Especially fun for anyone who likes pirate movies, but a supremely scenic mode of transportation for others! *FREE with Hakone Free Pass or 1000 yen one-way • Togendai, Hakonemachi-ko and Motohakone-ko*

Hakone Open Air Museum (箱根彫刻の森美術館)

A host of very imaginative and thought-provoking statues, sculptures and pieces of architecture, set in a lush, modern garden. The highlight, though, has to be the Picasso gallery, quite a rare collection outside Europe. *1600 yen (1400 yen with the Hakone Free Pass) • 9am-5pm • Chokokunomori station on Hakone Tozan Line*

Hakone Gora Park (箱根強羅公園)

Handily located next to a convenience store if you need some more supplies, this park has a western-inspired design. A good place to unwind and have a snack before continuing up the hill. *550 yen (free with the Hakone Free Pass) • 9am-5pm • Koenshimo station on cable car*

Hiking in Hakone

Around Komagatake and Hakone (駒ヶ岳+箱根山)

There are a few hiking courses around Mount Komagatake and Mount Hakone, which are the main mountains for tourists in Hakone. Note that due to seismic activity, routes can be closed off, so check with the tourism information centers when you get there and ask for their recommended routes. Hiking around Komagatake is an easy to access route, that takes visitors away from all the crowds and tour buses, and into a bit of nature with a closer look at some of the past volcanic activity. *Difficulty: Medium • Hike time: 2-6 hours, depending on route • Owakudani (ropeway) or Sounzan station (cable car)*

Old Tokaido Highway Hike

An old trading route through the forest to an ancient tea house, this is an uphill but enjoyable hike. Location well signposted from boat port and around, plus buses to take you back after. *Difficulty: Medium • Hike time: 2-3 hours • Moto-Hakone bus stop (routes K, H, Y)*

Cedar Tree Walk

A nice walk through an ancient cedar avenue, recommended for families or those that want a gentle walk, with no big inclines. *Difficulty: Easy • Walk time: Under 1 hour • Between the Hakone Sekisho and Hakone Detached Palace Garden on the main road. After exiting the carpark of Hakone Detached Palace Garden, take a left and walk down a bit. Entrance is on the right side.*

Recommended hot springs (温泉)

Tenzan Onsen (天山湯治郷 ひがな湯治 天山)

Inside a nice hotel, this hot spring has a traditional feel but all the facilities you would expect in a modern spa. *Adults 1300 yen, children 650 yen • 9am-11pm (reception closes at 10pm) • Hakone Tozan (K) bus to Okuyumoto-Iriguchi bus stop. You will see two roads heading off, take the winding road on the left (heading over the river)*

Yunessun (箱根小涌園 ユネッサン)

Not your average hot spring! This rather odd place features baths full of wine, sake or occasionally soda drinks to relax in. A good choice if you have already done an old-fashioned hot spring and want to try something a little crazy. *Adults 2900 yen, children 1600 yen • 9am-7pm • Short walk from Kowakidani station on Hakone Tozan Line*

Hotel Green Plaza (ホテルグリーンプラザ箱根)

Up in the mountains, with open-air baths that offer great views of Mount Fuji and the national park. Your skin will feel lovely and smooth due to the water's rich sodium bicarbonate content. *1600 yen • 3pm-midnight (Fri-Tue), 3pm-midnight (Wed, Thu) • Ubako station on ropeway*

Volunteer guides and tours

Odawara and Hakone Goodwill Guide Club - http://www.ohsgg.com/

Provides volunteer guide services in Hakone and the Odawara area.

Budget food

Eating out is often pricey here and most affordable accommodation comes with a shared kitchen, so most budget travelers should head to a convenience store near Yumoto-Hakone station. Otherwise there are a few reasonably-priced family restaurants near the station, but these do tend to close early. Remember it's legal to drink outside in Japan, so grab a beer from the store and chill out on the river!

Around Yumoto-Hakone station

Kanetsuki (加満幸) - Friendly atmosphere with Japanese set meals and soba, plus curry for kids and big kids alike. Plastic models outside makes it easy to order. *Soba from 600 yen • 11am-6pm • Opposite the station*

Heike (治兵衛) - Another nice joint for some simple hearty Japanese food. *Sets around 1000 yen • 11am-6pm • Further down the shopping street from Kanetsuki, on the left*

Cheap supermarkets (スーパー)

There's not really any cheap supermarket in central Hakone, but there is a supermarket in Odawara (station where your transfer for the train to Yumoto-Hakone station) called Odakyu OX (9am-9:30). Head out the east exit, through the bus terminal to the small triangular park in the road, then take the first right. There is also an A-Co-Op (A コープ) supermarket near Sengoku bus stop (9am-6pm), to the north west of central Hakone, which you can use the Hakone Free Pass to get to.

Water bottle refill spots

There are no water fountains on the hiking routes so it's best to go to a supermarket before and buy a large bottle or fill up your own one.

Shopping

Gotemba Premium Outlets

The most popular outlet mall for people living in Tokyo or Kanto, Gotemba has all the brands you could imagine. There are more than 200 stores in the complex, plus a food court and Ferris wheel. Prices are at least a bit lower than in the city and tax-free shopping is available. A must for shopaholics. *10am-8pm (Dec to Feb until 19:00) • Free shuttle bus from Gotemba station or take a bus to Gotemba Premium Outlets (included in Hakone Free Pass).*

Recommended cheap accommodation

Hostels and guest houses

K's House Hakone - Onsen Hostel

Cheap hostel chain, but this branch is a little different, with a modern hot spring and new, but traditional looking, architecture. Has a large kitchen and complimentary tea and coffee. *Dorms from 3500 yen*

Guesthouse Azito

Really great prices for private rooms at this guesthouse. This place has a bar to hang out in, plus a kitchen and Japanese tatami floors. *Single rooms from 3500 yen*

Campsites and mountain huts

Lake Ashinoko Camp Village (芦ノ湖キャンプ村)

Located on Lake Ashi (where the sightseeing cruises happen), this campsite is part of Fuji-Hakone National Park. Surrounded by trees, this campsite also has a restaurant, a small shop and a barbeque area. *Tent sites from 1000 yen, car sites from 3000 yen • Reception open 11am-5pm • Near Togendai-ko ropeway station •* http://campmura.com/ *(Japanese only)*

Getting around

The Hakone Tozan Train is a funny little train that takes you on a ride around and up the mountain in a zig-zagging fashion. The Hakone Ropeway and Hakone Tozan Cable car connect visitors with the Lake Ashi from the Hakone Tozan Line, offering stunning views over the mountains. All are included in the Hakone Free Pass, as is an easy-to-use bus network connecting the outlying settlements.

How to get there and away

From Shinjuku, take the Odakyu Line train to Odawara station, then the Hakone Tozan Line to Hakone-Yumoto station (90 mins).

Tourist information (観光案内所)

There is an excellent Odakyu Tourist Center in Shinjuku station, in the Odakyu Department Store building, near the Odakyu ticket gates (8am-6pm). There is also a tourist information center just outside Hakone-Yumoto station (9am-5:45pm).

Kamakura (鎌倉)

Kamakura is a great day trip from Tokyo, and when combined with the Enoshima Kamakura Freepass is a really cheap way to see a more traditional area. Most tourist spots are free or only a few hundred yen (or a somewhat pointless 20 yen for the giant Buddha!). Kamakura is full of interesting shrines, and great for autumn color and cherry blossoms. It can get awfully busy at weekends and on national holidays, so avoid these days if you can.

The Great Buddha of Kamakura, also known as Daibutsu

Discount pass: Enoshima Kamakura Freepass

Provides a round trip to Kamakura from Tokyo (Shinjuku station), as well as unlimited use of trains in the area for one day. There is a lot to do in Kamakura, and most of it is connected by the train lines of this pass. You will therefore start to save money very quickly. The cost of an Enoshima Kamakura Freepass is about the same as a return ticket. Buy from the Odakyu Sightseeing Service Center in Shinjuku station, or the Odakyu ticket machines in the station. The pass also provides discounts or free gifts at about 20 sites and restaurants in Kamakura. Check http://www.odakyu.jp/english/deels/freepass/enoshima_kamakura/ for the latest on offer. *Adults 1,470 yen, children 740 yen*

A little bit of history

Kamakura, a former capital of Japan, is an ancient city that was once as powerful as Nara and Kyoto. In 1192 warrior Minamoto Yoritomo established the first military government here, the Kamakura Bakufu. Previously the Imperial family in Kyoto held all power. The Hojo clan took over after Yoritomo's death and developed trade in the 13th century, importing Buddhism, Chinese lacquerware and Zen architecture, having a great effect on Japanese society. From the 17th century, Kamakura started to become more important as a temple city. After the war it also prospered as a popular getaway for Tokyoites, with its beaches, resorts and traditional districts.

Things to do

Daibutsu and Kotokuin Temple (大仏殿高徳院)

World Heritage-listed temple and grand Buddha bronze statue that visitors can walk up into. At a height of more than 13 meters and weighing in at about 121 tons, it's quite a sight. Be sure to have a look around the beautiful garden behind the Great Buddha to get your money's worth. *Adults 200 yen, children 150 yen, Grand Buddha 20 yen • 8am-5:30pm (Apr - Sept), 8am-5pm (Oct - Mar) • 10 mins north from Hase station on the Enoshima Electric Railway*

Tsurugaoka Hachimangu Shrine (鶴岡八幡宮)

The main shrine in Kamakura, another must see. In 1063, the Minamoto warrior clan created a power base around Kamakura after defeating clans to the north. The leader, Minamoto Yoriyoshi, returned to Kamakura and built this shrine near the coast to give thanks to the gods for his success. The Hachiman Kami (god) is therefore regarded as the protector of the warrior class. The result is a vast complex of well-maintained Japanese shrines, bridges and gardens. *FREE • 8:30am-4pm (24h at New Year) • 10 mins from Kamakura station, east exit*

Hasedera Temple (長谷寺)

Another must see in Kamakura, Hasedera is a significant Buddhist temple. It's said to have been here even before Kamakura was the capital in the Kamakura period (1185-1333). The temple has an 11-faced Kannon statue at around 10 meters tall, which is one of the largest wooden Buddha statues in Japan. The observation platform also has a good view of the town and sea to the south. *Adult 300 yen, children 100 yen (Treasure Museum + 200/100 yen) • 8am-5pm (Mar - Sept), 8am-4:30pm (Oct - Feb), Treasury 9am-5pm (closed Tuesdays) • Short walk from Hase station on Enoshima Electric Railway*

Zeniarai Benten Shrine
Something a little different here as statues and structures are in mini caves, or cut into the rock. Built in 1185 as a place for peace and quiet reflection, Japanese people come here to wash their money and pray for prosperity. Try this if you are a bit 'shrined out', or need somewhere to chill. *FREE • 8am-4:30pm • 20 mins walk from Kamakura station (west exit). Head down the main road leading from the station, through the tunnel, then follow the tourist signs*

Komachi Shopping Street
The main shopping street provides plenty of window shopping opportunities. There are lots of small, cheap Japanese candies to try as well, so as always be on the lookout for free samples! *From Kamakura station, head to the left of the east exit*

Kamakura Beaches
Picturesque beaches with greyish sand and rustic wooden buildings. Popular with surfers, there are stalls where visitors can rent out equipment and beach huts. Note that the beaches get extremely busy in summer. *FREE • South of Yuigahama station on the Enoshima Electric Railway*

Hiking trails
There are a variety of hiking trails accessible from nearby the train stations in Kamakura, with good signage in English.

Daibutsu hiking trail
Starting 350m down the road from Kotokuin Temple, this 3km trail is a nice way to escape the crowds and head up into the forests, passing the odd shrines and temple as you go. *Difficulty: Easy • Hike time: 1-2 hours*

Gionyama hiking trail
Shorter course on the east side, Gionyama also has a cave tomb to explore, in addition to nice views of the city. Considered the easiest hiking trail here. Starts from Myohonji Temple (妙本寺), a five-minute walk from Kamakura station, east exit. *Difficulty: Easy • Hike time: 30 mins*

Tenen hiking trail
Great hike up into the forested hills on the east side. There are several cave tombs along the way, plus this is the best trail to take during the autumn colors season. Most people start at Zuisen-ji Temple (瑞泉寺), 20 mins walk from Kamakura station, east exit (signs may point to Kamakura-gu Shrine first, which is on the way). *Difficulty: Easy • Hike time: 1-2 hours*

Volunteer guides and tours

Kanagawa Systematized Good Will Guide Club - http://www.ksgg.org/
A variety of tours available, such as a 4 hour walking tour to the main sites.

Budget food

On a hot day, getting something cheap from a supermarket or convenience store is best in Kamakura, as it's not as built up as some places. Sadly, the choice of budget restaurants is not as good as back in the big city. But there are still a few cheap restaurants around if needed.

Around Kamakura station

Saizeriya (サイゼリヤ) - Light Italian dishes, such as a small pizza or pasta dish, this is a good spot. *Pizzas from 390 yen, pasta from 399 yen • To the right side of the east exit • 10am-11pm*

Komachi Shopping Street

In addition to the traditional restaurants down this street, there are also some cheap chain restaurants. Expect some tourist prices here, so be warned! The following are in order from Kamakura station (Komachi Shopping Street is the street to the left from the east exit):

Kaiten Misakiko (海鮮三崎港) - Cheap conveyor belt sushi. *Sushi plate from 110 yen + tax*

Komachi Tonkatsu (小満ちとんかつ) - Opposite Kaiten Misakiko, this old school joint has some no fuss Japanese sets. Prices are not great, but this place is a nice way to try everyday Japanese sets. *Japanese sets from 980 yen*

Kamakura Rikyu (りきゅう) - Family run, casual budget Japanese restaurant with decent curries and other favorites. *Curry rice from 500 yen*

Cheap supermarkets (スーパー)

Tokyu Store (東急ストア) is located outside Kamakura station, east exit (9am-10pm), to the right.

Shopping

100 yen shops

Daiso (ダイソー) - In the shopping mall to the right side of Kamakura station, east exit. *9am-10pm*

Pharmacy (ドラッグストア)

Hac Drug Kamakura Shop (ハックドラッグ) is near Kamakura station, east exit. Head past the bus terminal, to the main road ahead, then down to the left a bit (9am-9pm).

Getting around

When you pick up your Enoshima Kamakura Freepass, be sure to take the free sightseeing map. This will show you how to get to each sightseeing spot. All the main sights are well signposted from the stations along this railway, as well as from Kamakura station, and are usually short walks away.

How to get there and away

From Shinjuku station, take the Odakyu Line to Fujisawa station, then the Enoshima Electric Railway to Enoshima station (76 mins, free with Enoshima Kamakura Freepass or 780 yen without).

Tourist information (観光案内所)

Inside Kamakura station (9am-7pm).

Kawagoe (川越)

Beautiful, traditional town less than an hour away from central Tokyo, in Saitama prefecture. It features a famous authentic old tower and shopping street, which is why many people call it 'Little Edo' (Edo was the old name for Tokyo). A great place for a nice one-day trip away from the skyscrapers of Tokyo. Kawagoe may not be as popular as other Tokyo side trips, but is still very much on domestic tourism maps.

Discount pass: Kawagoe Discount Pass

From Ikebukuro station in Tokyo, Tobu Railway offers the Kawagoe Discount Pass. It includes a return ticket, plus discounts or complimentary items at various stores in Kawagoe. It's a no brainer. At 700 yen for adults (360 yen for children), it is already cheaper than a return ticket. Available from the Tojo Line ticket offices of Ikebukuro station. The Kawagoe Discount Pass Premium is also available (adults 950 yen, children 480 yen), which additionally includes unlimited bus travel around Kawagoe on Tobu buses. It's not really required, unless you are really averse to lots of walking.

Things to do

Toki No Kane Bell Tower (時の鐘)

Still telling the time to residents, this is a traditional watch tower that is often featured in historical dramas. Kawagoe became a castle city in the 17th century (Edo period), and the feudal lord at the time ordered the grand bell tower to keep his subjects informed of the time. Would be crazy not to grab a photo of what is the icon of Kawagoe.

Kashiya Yokocho - Penny Candy Alley (菓子屋横丁)

Founded way back in the Meiji era, Kashiya Yokocho is a stone-paved alley lined with small shops selling nostalgic Japanese candy. Many of the candies are produced using the same processes as in the old days, and visitors can observe this process for free while strolling around. Small portions of these freshly made sweets are available as well, so try a few shops! As ever, keep a look out for free samples.

Kita-in Temple (喜多院)

A renowned temple only a short walk away from the other points of interest in Kawagoe. First built in 830, it features 540 stone Buddhas with various facial expressions, plus buildings and artifacts from castles in the Edo period. *Adults 400 yen, children 200 yen • Mon-Sat 8:50am-4:30pm, Sundays and holidays to 4:50pm (March 1 - Nov 23), Mon-Sat 8:50am-4pm, Sundays and holidays to 4:20pm (Nov 24 - Feb 28) (closed New Year holidays, Feb 2-3, Apr 2-5, Aug 16) • Down Toshogu Nakain Dori, follow tourist signs*

Volunteer guides and tours

The Kawagoe English Walkers - http://hebbon-juku.com/kawagoe-guide/
Local experts and English enthusiasts, ready to take you around and answer your questions. You just need to pay for your guides meal and expenses with this group.

Budget food

Wendy's First Kitchen (ファーストキッチン) - Cheap soups, burgers and pasta. *Pasta from 580 yen, burgers from 370 yen • 10am-9pm • Inside Hon-Kawagoe station. Also inside Atre Mall, outside Kawagoe station, east exit*
Hidakaya (日高屋) - Ramen and gyoza dumplings. *Ramen from 390 yen • 10am-3am • Outside Kawagoe station, west exit*
Kyotaru (京樽) - Cheap sushi shop. *Sushi from 108 yen • 11am-7pm • Inside Maruhiro Department Store (丸広百貨店), near the east exit of Hon-Kawagoe station*
Ootoya (大戸屋) - Japanese set meals. *Sets from 750 yen • 10am-10pm • Inside EQUIA(エキア) department store, Kawagoe station.*
Matsuya (松屋) - Rice bowls and curry. *Gyudon bowls from 290 yen • 24h • Just to the left of Kawagoe station, west exit. Also at Hon-Kawagoe station, east exit.*

Cheap supermarkets (スーパー)

There is a large supermarket in Tobu Store (川越マイン), the large building to the right of Kawagoe station, east exit (9am-1am).

Shopping

100 yen shops

Can Do (キャンドゥ) - Inside the Tobu Store complex, outside from Kawagoe station, east exit. *9am-9pm*
Watts (ワッツ) - Inside Hon-Kawagoe station. *10am-8pm*

How to get there and away

From Ikebukuro station (on the JR Yamanote Line), take the Tobu Line to Kawagoe (30 mins, 463 yen or free with Kawagoe Discount Pass).

Tourist information (観光案内所)

Inside Kawagoe station (9am-5pm).

Omiya and Bonsai Village (大宮)

Omiya, in Saitama prefecture, has a special place in many hearts as the often forgotten city in "that prefecture north of Tokyo". It may not be the coolest place on earth, but it's a great non-touristy day trip from Tokyo or a nice spot to stop off at on the Shinkansen if you have a bit of time left at the end of using a rail pass. The highlight here is the Bonsai Village, but Hikawa Shrine is also quite famous.

Things to do

Omiya Bonsai Village (大宮盆栽村)

Bonsai is the art of creating miniature tree sculptures, using painstaking work over many years to create stunning shapes and forms that the artist desires. While not often known to Tokyoites down south, Omiya Bonsai Village is known to Bonsai experts and Saitama residents to be the top site in Japan to see Bonsai trees. Great any time of the year, the village is full of many free to enter gardens, and the streets have been designed in a delightful fashion to show off the various Bonsai sites. You may even get to see the experts at work if you're lucky!

Omiya Bonsai Art Museum (大宮盆栽美術館)

An enthusiastic display of bonsai, and a must for flower enthusiasts or an interesting visit for those that want to know a little more about bonsai after visiting the surrounding gardens. The museum's aim is to promote the art and culture of bonsai, and it does this by displaying masterpieces from the area, including Ukiyoe woodblock paintings depicting bonsai. The history and process of making a bonsai tree is also explained in a series of galleries.

Adults 300 yen, high school to university age 150 yen, elementary to junior 100 yen • 10am-4pm (closed Thursdays and New Year holidays) • From Omiya, take the Tobu Urban Park Line to Omiya Koen station (4 mins, 150 yen). Alternatively, if coming from Tokyo on a JR train, you can continue on the Utsunomiya Line to Toro station • http://www.bonsai-art-museum.jp/en/

Walk it!

It's best to walk around the free bonsai gardens around the village first before considering the museum, as this is enough for most people. From Omiya Koen station, all the sights can be reached on foot, so just use the map to get to all the marked gardens. It is also possible to walk all the way to Omiya Koen station from downtown Omiya, via the below Hikawa Shrine. Just before the entrance to the shrine building, take a right turn and walk into Omiya Park. Head north up past the zoo and the lake, until you reach the exit after the racing center (大宮競輪場). Take a left around the middle school (さいたま市立大宮北中学校) and walk up to the station.

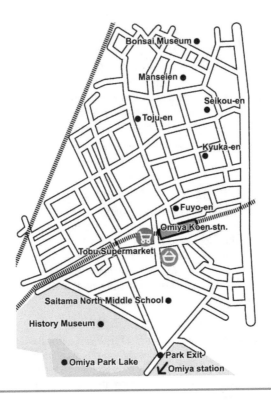

Omiya city

Hikawa Shrine (氷川神社)

Our favorite shrine in Saitama, and not a tour group in site to obstruct the view. This tranquil but impressive in size shrine has a history of more than 2000 years. The city got its name from the shrine, as Omiya actually means 'large shrine'. It is one of the top shrines in the Kanto region, so is a center for the faithful and a great spot for New Year celebrations. *FREE • Mar - Apr, Sept - Oct: 5am-5:30pm, May - Aug: 5am-6pm, Nov - Feb 6am-4:30pm • Head up the main road from Omiya station (east exit), past Takashimaya department store. Just before the police box and nearby 7-Eleven, you can see a wide path lined with trees. Head down here to the shrine (takes 15-20 mins in total)*

Railway Museum (鉄道博物館ミュージアムショップ)

A great place to geek out on trains or keep the children entertained on the super cute kiddie trains. There is a huge amount of history on show here, plus full sized trains of different generations to have a look around, including old Shinkansen trains. *Adults 1000 yen, elementary to high school age 500 yen, 3 and above 200 yen • 10am-6pm (closed Tuesdays and New Year holidays) • Head out of Omiya station west side, then follow the New Shuttle overhead tracks north (15 mins), or take the New Shuttle directly to Tetsudo-Hakubutsukan station (2 mins, 190 yen)*

Budget food

There are a few convenience stores in Omiya Bonsai Village to pick up take-away meals or snacks. If you are looking to eat in, there are a host of cheap places all around the Omiya station, but the best bet is to head up the shopping street to the left, after leaving Omiya station from the east exit. Here are some spots up this street (in order from station):

Yoshinoya (吉野家) - Gyudon eat-in and takeaway. *Meals from 330 yen • 24h*

Kaiten Misakiko (海鮮三崎港) – Cheap sushi. *Sushi plate from 110 yen + tax • 11am-10pm*

Ministop (ミニストップ) - Looks like a standard convenience store, but has a large takeaway menu for fast food cooked onsite. *Meals from 350 yen • 24h*

Matsuya (松屋) - Gyudon and burger eat-in and takeaway. *Meals from 290 yen • 24h*

Tenya (天丼てんや) - Cheap tempura (deep fried fish and vegetables) bowls and plates. *Bowls from 500 yen • 10:30am-10pm*

Hidakaya Ramen (日高屋) - Cheap ramen chain. Fried rice and gyoza dumplings also available. *Ramen from 390 yen • 10:30am-3am*

Cheap supermarkets (スーパー)

Daiei (ダイエー) is across from the west exit of Omiya station, and has a good selection for making your own food cheaply (9am-11pm). In the Bonsai Village, there is a Tobu supermarket just outside Omiya Koen station (6am-1am).

Shopping

100 yen shops

Daiso (ダイソー) - Located in Rakuun (ラクーン) shopping mall, which is up the shopping street on the left after exiting from Omiya station on the east side. There is also a Don Quijote variety shop here if you need more choice. *10am-9pm*

Pharmacy (ドラッグストア)

There is a large Sundrug (ドラッグストア) if you head out of Omiya on the east side and walk up the shopping street to the left. Open 10am-9:45pm.

How to get there and away

From Shinjuku station, take the **Saikyo Line** or Shonan-Shinjuku Line to Omiya station (30 mins, 470 yen). From Tokyo station, take the Utsunomiya Line to Omiya (30 mins, 550 yen) or just hop on the next north heading Shinkansen if using a rail pass. To get to Omiya Bonsai Village from Omiya, take the **Tobu Urban Park Line** to Omiya-Koen (3 mins, 150 yen). *Recommended rail passes: JR Tokyo Wide Pass, JR Rail Pass*

Tourist information (観光案内所)

There is a small tourist information booth in Omiya station (9am-7pm).

Kyoto

Kinkaku-ji, also known as the golden pavilion

Kyoto, the heart of traditional Japan, is a large city packed with countless amazing shrines and temples. The city has still retained much of its old-style atmosphere, due to strict building regulations and a traditionally-minded populace. It's a million miles away from the skyscrapers of Osaka and Tokyo. For first timers to Japan, it's a must to stay here for at least a day or two. For visitors who have already been before, there are still a host of lesser known and quieter spots to visit. The city has a grand total of 17 World Heritage sites, so people keep on coming back for more!

A little bit of history

Kyoto has been a prominent city since all the way back to the Nara period (AD 710 to 794), and since then has been seen as the cultural center of the country. It was the capital for around 1000 years before Emperor moved it to Tokyo. Much of the treasures and the rich culture from the ancient capital still remain today, in the shrines, temples, museums and Japanese gardens. Religious festivals, rituals and dances are still very much on offer, in events such as Gion Matsuri. In more recent years, it has made a name for itself in technology and is known as the hometown of gaming giant Nintendo, among others.

Highlights

1) Kinkaku-ji
You have probably seen the golden pavilion in postcards, and it's even more beautiful with your own eyes.

2) Kiyomizu-dera
Super popular temple, overlooking Kyoto and connected to a traditional shopping street.

3) Arashiyama
Kyoto's famous bamboo groves, possibly the best in Japan.

4) Fushimi Inari Taisha
Head up the mountains around Kyoto through hundreds of small red torii gates.

5) Gion
The place to see geisha, if you're super lucky!

Volunteer guides

Sakura Volunteer Guide Club - http://kyotofreeguide.web.fc2.com/
Well-respected club for volunteer guides, they can take you to major sites and tourist attractions with different plans available. One nice thing about this club is that for events, such as festivals, they organize special get-togethers for a small fee.

Good Samaritan Club - http://www.geocities.jp/goodsamaritanclub_hp/index.html
Another popular service, the members are local university students hoping to meet and show foreigners around. Usually one-day tours.

Goodwill Guide on Kyoto Handicraft & Historical Sites - http://ggkh.d.dooo.jp/
As the name suggests, this group focuses on traditional Kyoto, so is good for a more in-depth tour experience.

How to get there and away

By air
Kyoto doesn't have an airport, so the nearest international one is Kansai International Airport, near Osaka. From here there are cheap buses into Kyoto (90 mins, 2550 yen), which if you have lots of luggage may be better than local trains (95 mins, 1880 yen). Having said that, it may be worth getting an ICOCA and JR Haruka Pass. This combines use of a limited express train to and from the airport, plus a ICOCA card charged with 1500 yen. Available from 5200 yen for a round trip from the airport.

By train
Kyoto station is on the Shinkansen line, so use this if you have a Japan Rail Pass. There are frequent trains to Osaka and Nara. If you have a train pass, make sure you are using the correct lines. There are also frequent local trains to these nearby cities.

By bus

Many buses going from Tokyo to Osaka also stop in Kyoto, so they are a great option for budget travelers not using a Japan Rail Pass. Check prices at Japan Bus Lines, Willer Bus and JR Bus Kanto.

Discount pass: Kyoto City Bus One-Day Pass

With only two subway lines and a bunch of separate, expensive train lines, buses are the best way to get around Kyoto for budget travelers. While the buses can be slow, they link up with almost all the tourist spots in the city. This pass provides unlimited travel on the city buses for one day. Pass users will be saving money after just a few trips. Buy it from tourist information centers, such as in Kyoto station, or on any city bus. *Adults 500, children 250*

Sample itineraries

These itineraries can both be done with the bus pass:

Kyoto's best shrine and temples
This would be a great first day for visitors to Kyoto. Start off with a bang at Kiyomizu-dera, but head there as early as possible to avoid the crowds and see the amazing temple on the forested hill in peace. Next proceed up to Ginkaku-ji Temple, another world heritage site and enjoy a peaceful walk along the Philosopher's Walk. After lunch head to the west side for the breathtaking golden pavilion of Kinkaku-ji Temple and the surrounding temples.

Kyoto's special treasures
First, head to Shimogamo and Kamigamo shrines, to see some of the oldest, yet least visited of the main shrines in Kyoto. Then make your way south to Nijo castle and do some budget shopping and eating out in Kawaramachi Shopping District. In the evening head to Gion's southern streets to look out for geisha.

Cycle it and save!
Kyoto city has mainly flat, well maintained roads, so is perfect for bike riders. It can also be a way to avoid the sometimes frustratingly slow buses and lackluster subway system. Traveling from one side to the other would probably not take more than 1 hour, and there are excellent English language signs and maps everywhere, in case you get lost. Most good hostels or hotels will have bikes to rent out, or can suggest a nearby rental station. Renting from the place where you are staying is often cheaper.

Kyoto Budget Accommodation

Hostels and guest houses

Hannari

Our favorite in Kyoto by far. Spacious dorm booths keep the noise out, and there is a comfortable lounge downstairs to make friends and exchange travel tips. Free drinks and breakfast every day. *Dorms from 2500 yen •* http://hannari-guesthouse.com/

Kyoto Tomato Guest House

Cheerful hostel only a few minutes from Kyoto station. It therefore tends to get booked up early, so grab the chance if you can. Free wifi and cheap 100 yen washing machine. *Dorms 2300, Private rooms from 2700 yen •* http://kyoto.ihostelz.com/

Jiyujin

A little bit pricier than the others, but this definitely feels like a real Kyoto guesthouse, slightly rusting but with lots of charm. It's also smaller and therefore much quieter than the others. *Dorms 2600 yen, Singles 4000 yen, Twins from 3250 yen •* http://www.0757085177.com/

Internet cafes

topscafe (トップスカフェ)

Net cafe welcoming towards tourists. Rather basic, even for a net cafe, but has loads of free comics. If you use an app called Line, and become friends with topscafe (@topscafe-8), 100 yen discount may be available. *Night packs (ナイトパック) available from 9pm: from 1728 yen (+200 yen registration fee) • Opposite Kyoto Avanti shopping mall. Take the Hachijo east exit from Kyoto station, then walk across the road and the cafe is above the Nakau (なか卯) restaurant (2F) •* http://www.topsnet.co.jp/5/index.html

OWL (アウル)

Small net cafe with lots of cheap vending machines and a variety of seats and booths. Showers 500 yen. *Night packs (ナイトパック) available 9pm: from 2200 yen (weekends and holidays plus 500 yen) • Outside Hachioji exits, just down the narrow street at the Ibis hotel*

Kyoto city center and around Kyoto station (中心部)

In comparison to the rest of Kyoto, the city center has a large number of multi-storey buildings and department stores. It's not exactly Shibuya or Shinjuku, but it's the place to come for cheaper non-tourist priced shopping, travel supplies and the main location for transportation elsewhere. There are a few large temples within walking distance as well, so consider using the coin lockers in the station and having a walk around if you have some spare time before or after catching the train.

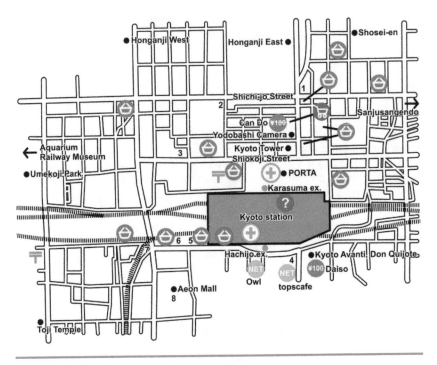

Things to do

North side

Honganji West Temple (西本願寺)

The headquarters of the largest school of Jōdo Shinshū Buddhism, Honganji was first established in 1321 but gained prominence in the 15th century. This growing power led it to be attacked multiple times, from rival sects such as Tendai and feudal lords such as Oda Nobunaga. The west temple is the largest of them all and the organization has now spread all over the world. Features include a Japanese garden, a worship hall called Amidado (Hall of Amida Buddha), the stunning Chinese-style cypress-thatched gate known as the Karamon and a large Ginkgo tree for autumn colors. *FREE • 5:50am-5:30pm (Mar - Oct), 6:20am-4:30 pm (Nov – Feb) • On foot: From Kyoto station Karasuma exit, head straight up Karasuma Dori, then take a left on the main road after Yodobashi Camera (Shichi-jo Dori). Walk until you reach the temple's moat. By bus: no.9 and 28 to Nishi Honganji-mae •* http://www.higashihonganji.or.jp/english_top/

Honganji East Temple (東本願寺)

Blighted by division and war over the centuries, the temples were broken apart in 1602 by a new Shogun called Tokugawa Ieyasu, splitting the sect's power base and leading to a more peaceful future. Best known for its massive Goei-dō gate that measures 27 meters high and 31 meters wide, the temple claims it's the largest wooden building in the world. *FREE • 5:50am-5:30 pm (Mar - Oct), 6:20am-4:30 pm*

(Nov - Feb) • On foot: From Kyoto station Karasuma exit, head straight up Karasuma Dori. By bus: no.5, 26, 88, 205, 206, 208 to Karasuma-Nanajo • http://www.hongwanji.or.jp/english/

Shosei-en Garden (渉成園)

Large garden, also known as Kikoku-tei, belonging to the Honganji East Temple. Built in the early Heian period (794-1185) and thought to be the former residence of the son of Emperor Saga. The Japanese pond is still the same as it was back then, and the serene garden was added in the 16th century by local noblemen. In addition, there are some tea houses and cherry blossom trees, so it can get pretty crowded in spring! *Entry by donation (500 yen recommended) • 9am-4pm • Quick walk east from Honganji East Temple*

Kyoto Tower (京都タワー)

Apparently the tallest non-steel reinforced tower (is that a good thing?!), Kyoto Tower is a rather dated building that provides a view of Kyoto and its surrounding mountains. It's not going to blow you away, but is worth it if you have time and some cash leftover. Otherwise, go to Fushimi Inari Taisha Shrine for a view over the city. *Adults 700 yen, junior high school students 550 yen, younger children 450 yen (minus 70 yen if you print out a discount coupon online at* https://www.keihanhotels-resorts.co.jp/kyoto-tower/coupon/, *if currently available. Use Google Translate, as the page is in Japanese) • 9am-9pm • Outside Kyoto station Karasuma exit*

South side

Toji Temple (東寺)

When Japan's capital was moved from Nara to Kyoto in 794, the west and east (Toji Temple) 'guardian temples' were built to protect Kyoto. The west temple no longer exists, but Toji remains to this day. Emperor Saga entrusted the temple to a monk named Kukai, who enlarged the complex with various halls, gardens and pagodas. Due to this illustrious history, it became a World Heritage listed Buddhist temple, famous for its grand five-storey, 54.8-meter high pagoda, which is the highest wooden tower in Japan. *Adults 500 yen, high school children 400 yen, elementary age 300 yen, infants free • 8:30am-5:00 pm (Mar 20 - Sept 19), 8:30 am-4:00 pm (Sept 20 - Mar 19) • On foot: take the Hachioji (south) exit and turn right. Walk down the road until you see a post office. Walk left down the main road, Toji is a minute down the road. By Bus: No. 202/208 to Toji Minamimonmae or No. 207 to Toji Higashimonmae. By train: Outside Toji station (Kintetsu Kyoto Line)*

East side

Sanjusangendo Temple

Completely breathtaking temple containing one thousand life-sized, golden Kannon statues in the world's longest wooden building, at 120 meters long. The main statue is of Kannon, a national treasure representing peace and compassion. Nothing quite like it. *Adults 600 yen, children 300 yen • 9am-4pm (Nov 16 - Mar 31), 8am-5pm (Apr 1 - Nov 15) • Hakubutsukan Sanjusangendo-mae on bus routes 100, 206 or 208. Also near Shichijo station on Keihan Line*

Walk/Cycle it and save!

To walk from Kyoto station to Sanjusangendo, take the Karasuma (north) exit and you will see Kyoto Tower. Walk down past Yodobashi Camera and then walk to the right on Shichi-jo street, walking over a river, until you get to Sanjusangendo Temple on the right. It takes about 20 minutes on foot.

Umekoji Park area (奈良公園)

A large playground and park on the west side of the station, great for families and big kids as well.

Kyoto Railway Museum (京都鉄道博物館)

Brand new museum showing off all the latest train technology, as well as in-depth exhibitions on railway history in Japan and abroad. The museum hosts plenty of hands-on experiences for all ages, from train simulators to model trains, plus visitors can ride on a steam train. Head there early in the day for a better chance of having a go on the main train simulators (visitors enter a draw on the second floor). *Adults 1200 yen, children 200-500 yen (10% off with Kyoto City Bus Pass, show on entry) • Open from 9:30am, closes 4:30pm (Nov - Feb), 5pm (Mar), 5:30pm (Apr - Sept), 5pm (Oct) • Bus no. 205, 206 to Umekoji-koen-mae, or 103, 104, 110, 86 or 88 to Umekoji-koen/Kyoto Railway Museum-mae •* http://www.kyotorailwaymuseum.jp/en/

Kyoto Aquarium (京都水族館)

Aspiring to be more than just an average aquarium, edutainment (education and entertainment) is the key word here. While there is somewhat of a focus on sea life around Kyoto, there are more exotic animals to see such as dolphins and seals. Interactive events and displays are numerous, so it's a good place to kill a few hours with the children. Save your money for the much larger aquarium in Osaka if also visiting there. *Adults 2050 yen, high school/uni students 1550 yen, junior/elementary 1000 yen, 3 and over 600 yen (10% off with Kyoto City Bus Pass, show on entry) • 10am-6pm • Short walk from Kyoto Railway Museum •* http://www.kyoto-aquarium.com/en/

Walk it and save!

It's possible to walk to the park in about 15-20 minutes from Kyoto station. Leave from the central exit (north side), walk over the bus terminal and take a left turn down the main road (Shiokoji Street). Walk 10 minutes to Umekoji Park (signposted along the way).

Budget food

North side of map

There are a bunch of cheap spots at Kyoto station's underground shopping mall on the north side. All sorts of food are available, from noodles to burgers. Note that there is also a supermarket in the Yodobashi Camera listed below. Above ground are the following cheap restaurants:

1) Sukiya (すき家) - Curry and gyudon eat-in and takeaway. *Meals from 360 yen • At the intersection of Shichi-jo Dori and Sarasuma Dori (north subway exits), just past the Yodobashi Camera up from the station • 24h*

2) **Nakau (なか卯)** - Cheap rice bowl chain, also has curry, soba and udon. *Bowls from 290 yen • To the west of the above Sukiya, down Shichi-jo Dori • 24h*
3) **Honke-kamadoya Bento (本家かまどや)** - Cheap bento takeaway shop. *Bento boxes from 300 yen • Down Shiokoji Dori street, after the post office and Lawson on the left • 10am-5pm*

South side of map

4) **Nakau (なか卯)** - Cheap rice bowl chain, also has curry, soba and udon. *Bowls from 290 yen. • Take the Hachijo east exit from Kyoto station, then walk across the road (opposite Kyoto Avanti shopping mall) • 24h*
5) **Yoshinoya (吉野家)** - Gyudon eat-in and takeaway. *Meals from 330 yen • From Hachijo exit take a right turn, Yoshinoya is just past 7-Eleven • 5am-2am*
6) **Yayoi Iken (やよい軒)** - Japanese teishoku (traditional set) meals. *Meals from 680 yen • Further down the road, past the above Yoshinoya • 7am-11pm*
7) **Tenkaippin (天下一品)** - Reasonably priced ramen, with various toppings and dumplings. *Ramen from 700 yen • Opposite the above Yayoi Iken • 11am-10pm*
8) **Marugame Udon (丸亀製麺)** - Simple udon bowls with lots of topping options. *Bowls from 290 yen • Aeon Mall (イオンモール KYOTO), down the road opposite the rail bridge near the above Yayoi Iken • 10am-10pm*

Water bottle refill spots

Apart from the bento shops, the above all have water jugs to refill your bottle. Kyoto Railway Museum and the aquarium also have water fountains.

Shopping

PORTA underground shopping mall (京都駅前地下街ＰＯＲＴＡ)

Large choice of restaurants and shops, from cheap soba joints to discount clothes shops. Includes a 300 yen shop called 3 Coins. *Head downstairs at the Karasuma (north) exit of Kyoto station.*

Yodobashi Camera (ヨドバシカメラ) with Uniqlo and supermarket

Huge electronics store with a Uniqlo for cheap clothes, offering tax-free shopping and with great multi-lingual support. Has a good section for foreign tourists, in case you lose that power adapter! There is also a large supermarket downstairs. *9:30am-10pm • Down Karasuma street (where Kyoto Tower is) after leaving from the Karasuma exit*

Cheap chain stores

Kyoto Avanti

A GU for clothes even cheaper than Uniqlo, plus some occasional deals to be found across the mall. *10am-9pm • Opposite the Hachijo east exit*

Don Quijote (ドン・キホーテ)

This crazily arranged megastore is full of any item you could imagine, from cheap souvenirs to fancy dress costumes to travel goods. Great prices and tax-free options available. *10am-midnight • Inside Kyoto Avanti*

100 yen shops

Daiso (ダイソー) - Great for cheap gifts. *10am-9pm • Kyoto Avanti*
Can Do (キャンドゥイ) - Larger than normal selection. *9:30am-10pm • Located in Yodobashi Camera*

Pharmacy (ドラッグ ストア)

Matsukiyo (薬 マツモトキヨシ) has a branch on the south side of Kyoto station. A Kokumin (コクミンドラッグ) is in PORTA shopping mall on the north side.

Tourist information (観光案内所)

Kyoto station has a superb information center, with a great selection of free maps and leaflets, plus a useful section showing local events and new deals.

Walk and save: Philosopher's Walk (哲学の道)

Ginkaku-ji on the Philosopher's Walk

Kyoto's quintessential walk, from Ginkaku-ji Temple in the north, down a quiet narrow canal and eventually to Nanzen-ji and surrounding temples. The canal is fed by Japan's largest lake, Lake Biwa, and is lined with cherry blossom trees in spring. It's lovely any time of the year though, with fireflies in the summer and autumn leaves in the fall. The route was given its name after Kitaro Nishida, a famous philosopher in the 19th century, who enjoyed walking through it as he developed his thoughts and theories. *Difficulty: Easy • Walk time: 30 minutes*

Sights along the walk

Signs along the way point out the below highlights, but don't be afraid to head off to some of the small, usually free temples and shrines that are dotted along the route. For some people, this may mean you only feel the need to pay for one or two of the highlights to feel satisfied on the temple's front.

Ginkaku-ji Temple (銀閣寺)

Ginkaku-ji (Temple of Shining Mercy) is a stunning Zen Buddhist temple and a highlight of any trip to Kyoto. Originally a grand retirement home, the site has now become a World Heritage site, best known for its so called iconic 'silver pavilion'. The traditional Japanese garden around the temple is full of interesting stone and gravel decorations, plus a 'wishing stone'. This temple could be considered the greatest example of Japanese traditional architecture. *Adults 500 yen, children 300 yen • 8:30am-5pm (Mar - Nov), 9am-4:30pm (Dec - Feb) • From Kyoto station, take the No.17 bus to Ginkakuji-michi. From other areas, take a bus to Ginkakuji-michi (No. 5, 17, 32, 100, 102, 203, 204)*

Honen-in Temple (法然院)

Founded in 1680 in recognition of Honen, the founder of a sect of Buddhism called Jodo. The perfectly maintained sand mounds inside are worth a look. A tranquil site, a little away from the main path, so often missed by some tourists. *FREE • 6am-4pm*

Eikando Temple (禅林寺)

The HQ of the Jōdo-shū sect, and formally named Zenrin Temple, was an important center of learning for Buddhists in Japan. Not completely essential, but the autumn leaves here are a must in the fall season. *Adults 600 yen, children 400 yen • 9am-5pm (gates close at 4pm)*

Nanzen-ji Temple (南禅寺)

Designated a Monument of Japan because of its beauty, Nanzen-ji Temple is one of the most well-known Rinzai Zen temple complexes in Japan. So admired by Emperor Kameyama in the 13th century, he built a palace here and after becoming a student of the local master, dedicated the palace as a Zen temple. Most of the areas in this complex have a charge, so best to just choose one or two, depending on your tastes. We recommend Nanzenin and the Hojo Rock Garden. Note that Nanzen-ji is also known as Zuiryusan. *Adults 500 yen, children 300 yen • No.5 bus to Nanzenji, Eikando-michi. 5 min walk from Kaege subway station*

Budget food

There are the odd old-fashioned cafes along the main route, and of course some vending machines (this is Japan!), but not much for budget travelers. Bring drinks and any snacks you need with you. The approach to Ginkaku-ji Temple, and to a lesser extent Nanzen-ji Temple, has plenty of small souvenir and ice cream shops, but not much in the way of cheap restaurants. There are also some convenience stores (コンビニ) near these starting points.

How to access the route

You can start at either Ginkaku-ji Temple or Nanzen-ji Temple, but from Ginkaku-ji Temple is much easier. Note that signs may say "Tetsugaku no michi", which is the Romanized version of the Japanese name for Philosopher's Walk. From Ginkaku-ji Temple, walk out of the main exit until you reach the narrow canal, which is the start of the walk. From Nanzen-ji Temple, head up Shishigatani Street (right from main entrance, then right again), and just past Eikando Temple (禅林寺) you will eventually see signs to the Philosopher's Walk (10 mins walk to start). *Recommended bus pass: Kyoto City Bus One-Day Pass*

Kinkaku-ji and surrounding temples (金閣寺)

Kinkaku-ji Temple (金閣寺)

If you were only going to see one temple in Japan, this World Heritage site would have to be it. Kinkaku-ji Temple, also known as the Temple of the Golden Pavilion, has become a symbol of Kyoto. Built in the 14th century as a villa for Shogun Ashikaga Yoshimitsu, it was subsequently converted into a temple after his death, as per his will. The beautiful temple is set in the Kyoko-chi pond, which is surrounded by a peaceful Japanese garden. The garden and pond are designed in a way so that the unusual shapes of the rocks and islands provide quite unique views of the temple from various angles. *Adults 400 yen, children 300 yen • 9am-5pm • Kyoto station, take the No.101 or 205 bus to Kinkakuji-michi. Also on routes 12, 59, 102, 204*

Ryoanji Temple (龍安寺)

Ryoanji Temple, meaning The Temple of the Dragon at Peace, is a World Heritage-listed "dry landscape" garden and temple. The mysteriously designed garden features large rock formations with pebbles raked in linear patterns to help in meditation. There are a few little temples around the large complex that are free to enter, plus a Japanese moss garden. *Adults 500 yen, children 300 yen • 8am-5pm (Mar - Nov), 8:30am-4:30pm (Dec - Feb) • No.59 bus to Ryoanji-mae*

Ninna-ji Temple (仁和寺)

The last temple in the chain, Ninna-ji was founded in 888 by the reigning emperor, but is now the headquarters of the Omuro sect of Buddhism. Highlights include a five-storey pagoda and elegantly painted Japanese doors and walls in the head priests building. The area also features buildings moved here in the 17th century from the Imperial Palace in Kyoto after a major fire, such as the Kon-do Hall (a National Treasure) and Meido Hall (an official Important Cultural Property). *Adults 500 yen, children 300 yen • 9am-5pm (Mar - Nov), 9am-4:30pm (Dec - Feb) • On bus routes No.10, 26 or 59 bus to Omuro Ninnaji*

Budget food

There are not too many budget options around the temples, apart from convenience stores or the odd mom and pop restaurant. Head downtown to the city center for more options.

How to get there and away

Use the Kyoto bus to get to the one of the bus stops mentioned above. *Recommended bus pass: Kyoto City Bus One-Day Pass*

Cycle it and save!

While it's a bit of a walk, it is perfectly possible to cycle down Hontsuji Dori (Street) and Kinuake-No-Michi, which connect all these temples. The temples are listed above in order along the street, and the whole cycle route takes only 10-15 minutes along flat road. Continue another 15 minutes to the west and you will also get to Arashiyama.

Kiyomizu-dera (清水寺)

One of the most celebrated Buddhist temples in Kyoto and a UNESCO World Heritage site. Its most famous section, the grand hall, is supported by 139 huge pillars overhanging a cliff. It offers great views of the city and surrounding Buddhist structures. There is a small three-storey pagoda, plus gardens and woods in the temple complex to explore. Also, try out the wish-granting Otowa waterfall! Unfortunately, in recent years the temple can seem very crowded, so come in the early morning/sunrise for a stunning photo of Kiyomizu-dera, without too many large tour groups blocking your path. *Adults 300 yen, children 200 yen • Usually 6am-6pm • City Bus: From Kyoto station, take No.100 or 206 buses to Gojozaka. Also on bus no. 202, 207 • Recommended bus pass: Kyoto City Bus One-Day Pass*

Fushimi Inari Taisha (伏見稲荷大社)

The head shrine of more than 30,000 across Japan, Fushimi Inari Taisha is an iconic shrine complex running up a steep mountain, best known for its countless number of red 'torii' gates. Established in 711 AD, it attracts believers who come here to pray for good harvests and prosperity in their businesses. Be sure to walk through the hundreds of red gates that take you up the mountain, giving visitors an awesome view of Kyoto from above.
FREE • 24h • Bus: No.5 bus to Inaritaisya-mae. Train: From Kyoto station, take the Nara Line to Inari station (140 yen, 6 mins) • Recommended bus pass: Kyoto City Bus One-Day Pass

Nijo Castle (二条城)

Built by the Shogun ruler of Japan in the 17th century, Tokugawa Ieyasu, Nijo Castle is another UNESCO World Heritage site and a must see in Kyoto. While much of it was destroyed by fire in 1750, many of the impressive structures and a lovely Japanese garden remain to this day. Also of interest are the sliding paper doors of the rooms, meticulously decorated with paintings from legendary Japanese artists. Come early in the day to avoid the tour buses. *FREE • 24h • Bus: No. 9, 12, 50 or 101 to Nijojo-mae. Subway: From Kyoto station, take Karasuma Line to Karasumaoike, then the Tozai Line to Nijojo-mae (140 yen, 6 mins) • Recommended bus pass: Kyoto City Bus One-Day Pass*

Gion (祇園)

An excellent example of downtown Kyoto, Gion is full of wooden teahouses and traditional townhouses. For people seeking the atmosphere of old Kyoto, Gion is perfect. Maiko, trainee geisha, are known to walk around the area as well, commuting to perform for the rich and famous. Even if you don't get to see a geisha, Gion still offers a cheap afternoon or evening.

Things to do

Traditional areas

As you walk around Gion, there are a few areas and streets that every visitor needs to see. The **Shirakawa** area has a relaxing, shallow canal running down it, with amazingly pristine and well maintained wooden stores and other establishments. **Hanami-koji,** on the south side, is your best bet for seeing geisha. If you are lucky you will see one walking around, but be discreet as they are often harassed by tourists. Just have that camera ready when you are walking around, just in case! Best time to see them is in the evening.

Minami-za Kabuki Theater

Performances here are quite pricey for Kabuki (ancient Japanese theater), but it's sometimes possible to have a little look inside. Note that construction work may be in progress while you are in Kyoto, but it's still definitely worth checking it out. The classical Japanese building is definitely worth a photo.

Yasaka Shrine

Originally built way back in 876 and the headquarters for thousands of other shrines, Yasaka is a big complex of well maintained, stunning shrines, pagodas and other Shinto monuments and buildings. Locals used to refer to it as Gion-sha (meaning 'Gion's Shrine'), due to its significance to the area. *FREE • 10am-5pm*

Walk it and save!

It's a bit difficult to know exactly where to go, so follow our handy walking route on the map to see all the highlights.

Budget food

The restaurants can be expensive here, it's best to walk for a few minutes west to the shopping district around Kawaramachi station if you want to eat inside. There is a large collection of cheap restaurants there.

Budget chain restaurants on map

1) Tenkaippin (天下一品) - ramen. *Ramen from 700 yen • 11am-3am*

Cheap supermarkets (スーパー)

Fresco (フレスコ 祇園店) is open 24h, near Gion-Shijo station.

Shopping

100 yen shops
Lawson 100 (ローソンストア 100) - North of the Shirakawa area. *24h*

Pharmacy (ドラッグストア)
Daikoku Drug Store also has snacks and drinks for 100 yen (11am-10pm).

How to get there and away

By bus
City Bus routes no. 12, 46, 100, 201, 202, 203, 206 or 207. From Kyoto station, take the 205 bus to Shijo Kawaramachi, then walk east across the bridge. *Recommended bus pass: Kyoto City Bus One-Day Pass*

By rail
The nearest train station is Gion Shijo station on the **Keihan Main Line**.

Arashiyama (嵐山)

A very popular tourist spot in Kyoto, probably best known for its monkey park and bamboo groves. But there is a lot more to see here, from countless temples to souvenir shops to stunning mountain scenery. You can easily spend a whole day here, and it's all very walkable for budget travelers.

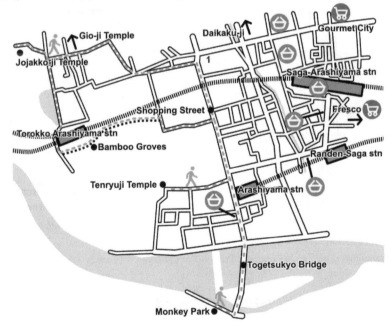

Walk it and save!

The Arashiyama area in general makes for a nice stroll, so follow our recommended route to see a few extra hidden treasures. Head down any side streets that look of interest, as there are many small shrines and temples dotted around. Most are free!

Things to do

Arashiyama Monkey Park Iwatayama (嵐山モンキーパークいわたやま)

A fun little experience, especially for the children, this park is located up a hill on Oi River and is home to many funny Japanese macaque. There is a short hike up to the top, which provides a superb view over the city, plus wild deer if you are lucky. At the top visitors can feed the monkeys. *Adults 550 yen, children 250 yen, under 4s FREE • 9am-5pm (until 4pm Nov 1 - Mar 14) • South of Togetsukyo Bridge*

Togetsukyo Bridge (渡月橋)

A good way to get a view of the scenic forested hills, this 155-meter bridge over the Katsura River is worth a quick visit. The bridge may have concrete legs, but the wooden surface still makes for a pretty awesome picture. *FREE • South of Arashiyama's shopping street*

Tenryuji Temple (天龍寺)

Yet another UNESCO World Heritage site for Kyoto, this temple is rather spread out, but fun to navigate complex. It houses a beautiful pond surrounded by well-manicured gardens and stone decorations. Originally founded as Japan's first Zen Buddhist temple, it was eventually abandoned before becoming used by emperors to reside in, before returning to its original religious purpose again. It's recommended to pay a little extra to go inside the temple buildings as well, as this costs only a few more dollars. *Gardens: Adults 500 yen, children 300 yen, preschool FREE (+300 yen for buildings. Save by buying at same time) • 8:30am-5:30pm (until 5pm Oct 21 - Mar 20) • Bus No.11, 28 or 93 to Arashiyama Tenryuji-mae*

Arashiyama Bamboo Groves (竹林の道)

It's quite a mesmerizing experience walking through this sprawling bamboo grove, and not hard to see how it became one of Kyoto's top budget travel spots. The Arashiyama Bamboo Groves makes for a nice walk for people who want to experience the quiet, traditional side of Japan. One of Kyoto's most picturesque locations. *FREE • 24h • Just north of Tenryuji Temple*

Jojakko-ji Temple (常寂光寺)

Less crowded than most in the area, this small temple is a relaxing retreat. There is a quaint little pagoda, plus some good spots to sit down after all that walking around. *500 yen • 9am-5pm • Just north of the bamboo grove*

Northern temples

Discount pass: Shared Admission Ticket
Save 200 yen by getting this ticket at one of the two spots below. This ticket allows access to both, which are 25 minutes on foot from each other.

Gio-ji Temple (祇王寺)

Surrounded by a bamboo grove, a moss covered garden and maple trees, this tiny thatched roofed temple is a nice excuse for a walk into the traditional suburbs north of Arashiyama. While the size means there is less to do and see than other temples, it has become a favorite for many living in Kyoto. *Adults 300 yen, children 100 yen • 9am-5pm • 10 mins north of Jojakkoji*

Daikaku-ji Temple (大覚寺)

Daikaku-ji is a quiet temple in northern Kyoto, away from the crowds of central Arashiyama. The site was first established more than 1200 years ago as an Imperial villa, and in the past head priests were from the imperial family. Just behind Daikaku-ji Temple is the free Gosha-myojin Shrine (五社明神), a distinctive, yet slightly run down Buddhist site. *Adults 500 yen, children 300 yen • 9am-5pm • Bus No.28 or 91 to Daikakuji. 25-minute walk from central Arashiyama*

Free sample heaven

Arashiyama Shopping Street

While around Togetsukyo Bridge can feel like it's full of selfie-taking tourists, if you head up the road from Tenryuji Temple there are lots of shops to enjoy. Many of these have free samples to try out, so you don't have to spend lots of money.

Budget food

The budget chains are pretty non-existent around this staunchly traditional area, but that doesn't mean a budget traveler should be lost for options. In addition to two large supermarkets (and of course convenience stores) and the odd takeout, there are some slightly pricey Japanese mom and pop restaurants if you want to treat yourself to an authentic Japanese meal. Hokka Hokka Tei (ほっかほっか亭) is a cheap bento box takeout, with special lunch deals. *Bentos from 390 yen*

Cheap supermarkets (スーパー)

Gourmet City supermarket (グルメシティ) is down Maruta-Machi Street (9am-9pm). Another option is Fresco (フレスコ), which has slightly lower prices (9am-9pm).

Water bottle refill spots

While there are few clean water fountains, visitors can usually pick up small, free drink samples from the shopping streets.

How to get there and away

If you just want to spend the day here, walking around the sites, then getting the train, rather than the bus, would be cheaper and quicker. From Kyoto station, take the JR Sagano Line to Saga-Arashiyama (16 minutes, 240 yen). Otherwise, use the directions above to head to one of the main sites via bus, from where you can continue on foot. *Recommended bus pass: Kyoto City Bus One-Day Pass*

Kawaramachi Shopping District (河原町)

Kawaramachi is our favorite place to come for a spot of budget shopping in Kyoto, as well as being a great hub to stop off at for a cheap meal. In addition to these modern delights around the station is the lively downtown market called **Nishiki Market**. Known as a place to find Kyoto's most famous fish, snacks and other various goods, the long, 'keeping it simple' street is fascinating. Prices can be reasonable, but look around before purchasing as there is much on offer. Also worth checking out is **Pontocho Alley**, an atmospheric street running parallel to Kamogawa river. No modern buildings or signs are allowed here, just like Gion. Head there in the evening, especially on Friday or Saturday when there is more chance of seeing Maiko (trainee Geisha).

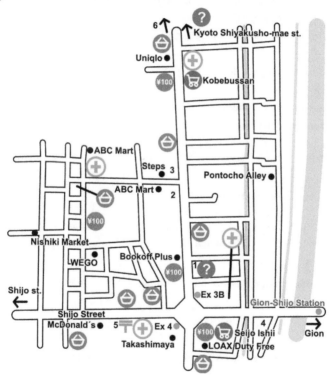

Budget food

Budget restaurants

1) Ringer Hut (リンガーハット) - fish ramen. *Ramen from 630 yen • 11am-2am*
2) Kappa Sushi (かっぱ寿司) - conveyor belt sushi. *Sushi from 108 yen • 11am-10pm*
3) Matsuya (松屋) - rice bowls and curry. *Gyudon bowls from 290 yen • 24h*
4) Sukiya (すき家) - gyudon and curry. Bowls from 360 yen • 24h

5) **Mos Burger (モス)** - Japanese burgers. *Burgers from 220 yen • 7am-midnight*

6) **Yayoi Iken (やよい軒)** - Japanese sets. *Meals from 680 yen • 24h*

Cheap supermarkets (スーパー)

Cheapest is Kobebussan (業務スーパー), open 10am-10pm. Nearer the station, the pricier Seijo Ishii (成城石井) has a good range of foreign goods and bakery items (8am-10pm).

Shopping

LAOX Duty Free (ラオックス)

Specializing in tax-free shopping for foreign tourists, LAOX has everything from cosmetics to suitcases to electronics. *10:30am-8:30pm • Marui Department Store*

Bookoff Plus (ブックオフ)

Great spot for second hand books, DVDs and CDs. *11am-10pm*

Uniqlo (ユニクロ)

Local branch of the mega budget clothing brand. *11am-9pm*

WEGO (ウィゴー)

Discount clothes shop for youth fashion. *11am-8:30 pm*

ABC Mart (ABC マート)

A few branches of the discount shoe shop are in the area, with prices sometimes as low as 1000 yen. Steps is also worth checking out for cheap shoes. *11am-9pm*

100 yen shops

Plenty near Kawaramachi station:

Daiso (ダイソー) - Two on the west side. *10am-9pm*

Seria (セリア) - Inside Marui Department Store, exit 3A. *10:30am-8:30pm*

Can Do (キャンドゥイ) - Top of map. *10am-10pm*

Pharmacy (ドラッグストア)

There are various pharmacies around Kawaramachi station, most open 10am-10pm.

How to get there and away

On foot or bicycle

Gion is a few minutes away, as is Shijo station on the subway line. Kyoto station is about 35-minute walk away on foot, to the south.

By bus

Bus no. 4, 5, 10, 11, 12, 17, 32, 46, 59, 201, 203, 205, 207. From Kyoto station get bus no. 4 (fastest), 17 or 205. *Recommended bus pass: Kyoto City Bus One-Day Pass*

By rail

From Kyoto, take the Kyoto Subway Karasuma Line to Shijo station, then the Hankyu Kyoto Line to Kawaramachi station (13 mins, 360 yen). It's also quite possible to just take a 10-minute walk from Shijo station (saves 150 yen).

Tourist information (観光案内所)

Travel agent H.I.S (9am-6pm) has a branch near the Kawaramachi station, but the official tourist information center is up the road (8:45am-5:30pm, closed weekends).

Shimogamo and Kamigamo Shrines

Shimogamo Shrine

These two partnered World Heritage shrines are away from most of the crowds, and most importantly free!

Kamigamo Shrine (上賀茂神社)

The oldest Shinto shrine in Kyoto, and still of great significance to followers. Kamigamo, a shrine dating from the Heian period, is known across the country for its iconic sand cones. The shrine is also surrounded by a picturesque primeval forest, featuring large Japanese oak trees and weeping cherry trees. There is a supermarket and convenience store just across the bridge, if you need any cheap snacks or drinks. *FREE • 5:50am-5pm • City Bus: No.4 or 46 to Kamigamojinja-mae*

Shimogamo Shrine (下鴨神社)

Also one of the oldest shrines in Japan, with construction thought to date back to the 6th century. Has a similar style to Kamigamo, called 'nagare-zukuri' (flowing style), with the complex comprising dozens of small shrine buildings. Once you have done the main area, walk south through the forest (Tadasu no Mori), the last remaining section of the Yamashiro Plains. At the end are some more free shrines, often missed by tourists, but a lovely place to retreat to. *FREE • 5:30am-6pm (summer), 6:30am-5pm (winter)• City Bus: From Kyoto station, take bus no. 4 to Shimogamojinja-mae. Also on bus no. 205 • Recommended bus pass: Kyoto City Bus One-Day Pass*

Osaka

Dotonbori Street, Namba

Spiritually the southern capital of Japan, Osaka is the business and entertainment center of the south. Osaka is not the most exciting city in the world, and for most people Tokyo has much more to offer. But there still come cool places to check out in Osaka, and it's interesting to compare the two big cities. It's also in a perfect location from which to base further travels into the Kansai region, such as to Kyoto, Nara and Kobe, on a budget.

A little bit of history

When Chinese culture was first introduced into Japan in the 5th century, Osaka became an important location in politics, culture and business. The capital was built here in the 7th century, but moved to Nara and then Kyoto in subsequent years. The city still continued to flourish as a place to do business. Osaka became known as the merchant city, while Tokyo eventually became the center for politics and government when the capital moved there in the 17th century. It has made Osaka people into arguably friendlier, more open people than their northern neighbors.

Highlights

1) Kuromon Market (Namba)
See how Japanese people used to shop at this staunchly traditional market.

2) Osaka Aquarium Kaiyukan
Fun place to take the children, but the sheer size of it all means there is something for everyone here.

3) Den Den Electric Town (Namba)
The main electronics district, with lots of gaming arcades and tax-free shopping.

4) Amemura (Namba)
Osaka's fashion town, full of new styles and a few bargains.

5) Minoo Park
A lovely, quiet retreat from central Osaka. Great hiking opportunities and no crowds.

6) Dotonbori (Namba)
The main entertainment and eating area in Osaka. Full of atmosphere, with a stunning canal. Best in the evening.

Volunteer Guides

Osaka SGG Club - http://fgnosa.sakura.ne.jp/
Guides from this club are able to take visitors to the main sites, as well as nearby cities such as Nara and Kyoto. They like to show off both modern and old areas of each area.

Visit Kansai - http://www.visitkansai.com/
For those visiting places such as Osaka, Kyoto or Nara, Visit Kansai is a great choice. They have loads of bubbly volunteer guides who want to give tourists a real behind-the-scenes experience.

IC cards

There are various IC cards, but the most popular is ICOCA. Similar to the Suica card in Tokyo, it can be used on bus and trains in Osaka. It helps to reduce the hassle and difficulty of buying individual tickets, but the 500 yen deposit will probably eliminate any savings if just using it for a day or two. Note that ICOCA and Tokyo's Suica cards now work on each other's networks. Available from JR ticket machines. *2000 yen (500 yen deposit, 1500 yen put on card)*

124

How to get there and away

By air

The main airport for international flights is Kansai International Airport. There are cheap buses into town, but taking a train is much easier. The Nankai and JR train lines both go to Osaka city for around 1000 yen. Use Hyperdia to see which is cheaper to your accommodation. Note that there is also a combined ICOCA and JR Haruka Pass available exclusively to tourists. It combines use of a limited express train to and from the airport, plus an ICOCA card charged with 1500 yen. *Available from 4200 yen for a round trip from the airport. Each use of the limited express is from 1710 yen, so good savings can be made.*

By train

If you are far from Osaka and have the Japan Rail Pass, you should take the Shinkansen to Shin-Osaka station. Otherwise, take normal trains to Osaka, Umeda or Namba stations, the main ones in the city center. There are frequent services to Kyoto and Nara.

By bus

Osaka is the main transportation hub in Kansai. If you don't have a Japan Rail Pass, there are cheap buses available from other major cities, such as Tokyo or Hiroshima. Check prices at Japan Bus Lines, Willer Bus and JR Bus Kanto.

Discount transportation passes

Also consider the Osaka Kaiyu Ticket if going to the aquarium.

Osaka Visitors' Ticket

Unlimited rides on all Osaka municipal buses, subway lines and trams for one day. It will get you to almost all the spots in this guide, with the exceptions of Sumiyoshi Taisha Shrine and Minoo Park. The super low price for foreigners makes this pass a no-brainer. Available at the tourist information centers at Kansai airport and Shinsaibashi in Namba, as well as travel agents abroad. A tourist visa is required, so bring your passport. *Adults 550 yen (adults only)*

Enjoy Eco Card

Same as the Osaka Visitors' Ticket, but does not require a tourist visa, so good for students and those living in Japan. Also note that as there are no Osaka Visitors' Tickets available for children, getting an Enjoy Eco Card for them is cheaper. *Adults 800 yen, children 300 yen*

Osaka Amazing Pass

In addition to the features of the other passes, this one also allows travel on the private rail lines in Osaka (only excluding JR lines), if using just for one day. The two-day Osaka Amazing Pass has no additional transportation features. What sets this pass apart is that it includes free access to 35 tourist spots, including the Osaka Castle museum, and a large coupon book for additional discounts and benefits at countless more. Generally, if you were to cram in a few of the included attractions, you could save money, but quite a lot of them are not what most would call Osaka's star attractions. Have a look at the current line-up at https://www.osaka-info.jp/osp/en/ to see if it's worth it. Purchase at tourist information centers and stations in Osaka. *1 day 2500 yen, 2 days 3300 yen (no child prices)*

Sample itinerary: Osaka in a day
In the morning, start by checking out the old-school Kuromon Market, then pop over to the grand aquarium, one of Japan's best. In the afternoon head to Namba for some evening shopping and the vibrant nightlife of Dotonbori. If you have time, check out Shinsekai, full of bright lights and noisy bars to enjoy. Best done with the Osaka Visitors' Ticket or the Enjoy Eco Card, to save a bit of money.

Osaka Budget Accommodation

Just like its big brother Tokyo, Osaka has a host of options for those on a budget. Here are the highlights:

Hostels and Guest Houses

Shin-Osaka Youth Hostel
A new youth hostel, right next to the Shinkansen station for Osaka (Shin-Osaka station). Japanese and western style rooms available. *Dorms from 3500 yen •*
http://osaka-yha.or.jp/shin-osaka-eng/

J-Hoppers Osaka Guesthouse
A highly rated hostel near Umeda station. Lots of free services, a big kitchen so you can cook for yourself and cheap bike rental services. *Dorms from 2700 yen •*
http://osaka.j-hoppers.com/

Bonsai Guest House
A nice little guest house not far from the main sights of Osaka. Japanese and western style rooms available. Comes highly recommended. *Dorms from 2800 yen •*
http://www.bonsaiguesthouse.com

Hostel 64 Osaka
More modern hostel, within walking distance of many tourist spots in Osaka. Also has lots of services available, like bike rentals. *Dorms from 3500 yen •*
http://hostel64.com/

Love hotels (adults only)

The following, plus an increasing number of other love hotels, are bookable at Booking.com.

Hotel Fine Garden

A national chain of 'adult only' hotels, this branch is near Umeda station. Colorful and fun! *Rooms from 3584 yen*

Hotel La Aroma Tennoji

Another 'adult only' hotel in central Osaka, but this one seems a bit more stylish and upmarket. For one night only! *Rooms from 8064 yen*

Capsule hotels

Capsule Hotel Asahi Plaza Shinsaibashi

Not exactly a five-star hotel, but this capsule hotel is fine for a few days. Good English support and free spa access included. *Capsules from 2900 yen • See Namba map •* http://www.asahiplaza.co.jp

B&S Eco Cube Shinsaibashi

Modern, clean capsule hotel with a ladies-only floor. Free Wi-fi and PC use. *Capsules from 2500 yen • See Namba map •* https://eco-cube.jp

Capsule Inn Osaka (men only)

Not as modern or clean as the others, but has the lowest prices and is close to Umeda station. *Capsules from 2400 yen • From Exit M2 of Umeda, walk 3 mins east along shopping arcade •* http://www.capsulehotel-inn-osaka.com

Overnight Spas (super sentos)

Spa World (スパワールド)

This huge spa and entertainment complex also allows visitors to stay a night, on lazyboy chairs or on Japanese tatami floors. Hotel style rooms also available. *1300 yen extra •* http://www.spaworld.co.jp/english/

Internet cafes

Aprecio (アプレシオ)

Well run comic cafe with a good selection of cheap meals and ice creams. Also accepts credit cards and has a ladies-only area. *Night pack (ナイトパック) available from 9pm: 6 hours (6 時間ナイトパック) from 1760 yen, 9 hours (9 時間ナイトパック) from 2480 yen • See Namba map*

MediaCafe Popeye (メディアカフェポパイ)

Loads of these around Osaka. A safe option, this chain is well accustomed to foreign tourists staying. Usual selection of free comics and drinks. *Night pack (ナイトパック) available from 10pm: 5 hours (5 時間ナイトパック) from 980 yen, 10 hours (10 時間ナイトパック) from 1860 yen • See Namba map*

Namba (難波)

Bustling, bright and always energetic, Namba is what most people imagine a Japanese downtown is like. The area is full of never-seen-before sites and hidden alleyways to explore on foot, making it a perfect holiday spot for budget travelers. There are countless shops, bars, cafes and more here, so give yourself at least an afternoon or two to enjoy all the sights.

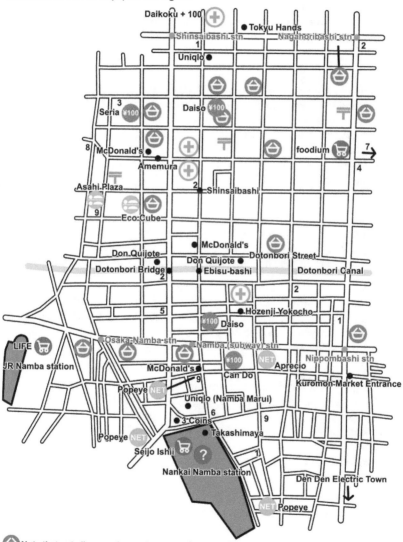

Note that not all convenience stores are shown on this map, due to the vast numbers.

Things to do

Dotonbori Street (道頓堀)

You have probably seen a picture of the Glico boy and the bright neon lights along Dotonbori canal, and if you have not you will definitely remember it after visiting. This is the main place to go for drinks or food in the evening in Osaka. It's full of reasonably priced restaurants and bars, and has a lively character that will force you to get out your camera and take a few pics! Just be sure to avoid bars that have cover charges. There are plenty without, and signs outside usually say if there is a cover/table charge. Say "charji arimas ka?" to a member of staff to check if you are worried. *Just north of the Namba stations, on the canal*

Kuromon Market (黒門市場)

With nearly 200 years of history, this vibrant 600-meter long market is a great place for a free stroll and a bit of window shopping. Known as "Osaka's Kitchen" by locals, there seems to be an endless supply of strange and interesting little shops run by local residents. The 150-plus shops mainly sell fish, meat and vegetables, but an increasing number are now catering to travelers with simple takeout dishes such as sushi, sashimi and grilled fish. Best to come in the morning, when it's livelier. *Two-minute walk from Nippombashi station*

Hozenji Yokocho (法善寺横丁)

A few narrow, stone paved streets near the local Hozenji Temple, this area feels like Osaka before the bright lights of Dotonbori. Small restaurants and cafes line the lovingly quaint streets. The free temple and its moss-covered statue Buddhist statue are worth checking out. *One-minute from Namba Subway station (near exit 14)*

Den Den Electric Town (でんでんタウン)

Den Den Electric Town is Osaka's answer to Akihabara. The area is packed with huge electronic shops selling anything you can imagine, maid cafes, game arcades (most games still just 100 yen a play) and lots of other exciting 21st century attractions. *Just walk five minutes down from Nippombashi subway station*

Shinsaibashi (心斎橋)

While not quite as down to earth and authentic as the other shopping and eating spots, Shinsaibashi and the covered shopping arcades do tend to get lower prices. Osaka's largest shopping area is always heaving with people, and is full of all kinds of shops and restaurants. *From Namba Subway station, take exit 14 or 15B, then walk north towards the canal. Take a right into Dotonbori Street just before the canal, then take the first left (you will see a dancing crab model). Walk over the bridge to arrive at the entrance*

Amemura (アメリカ村)

Osaka's youth town, Amemura is rich with Japan's take on American culture, sometimes amusing and odd, sometimes super tasty. It all started in the 1970s, when warehouses in the areas started selling imported goods from the US, such as jeans, records and music. It eventually grew to become a spot to break new fashion, media and entertainment trends in Japan. A cool spot for a bit of people watching. *Between Shinsaibashi and Namba subway stations*

Walk it and save!

Once you get to one of the Namba stations (JR Namba, Osaka-Namba, Namba...yes it's confusing), use one of the station maps and the one in this chapter to get your bearings. From here everything is within walking distance. Walking down Dotonbori Canal in the evening with a drink or two is a cheap way to spend a fun evening. Osaka people are known to be friendly, so you may make some new friends!

Free sample heaven

Takashimaya Food Court (大阪高島屋)
This posh underground food court has products that are way out of most people's price range, but walk around to pick up some free samples of the latest confectionery or breads. *10am-8:30pm • B1 of Namba City, in Namba station*

Budget food

Budget restaurants on map

1) Matsuya (松屋) - rice bowls and curry. *Gyudon bowls from 290 yen • 24h*
2) Yoshinoya (吉野家) - gyudon and curry. *Bowls from 330 yen • 24h*
3) Mos Burger (モス) - Japanese burgers. *Burgers from 220 yen • 7am-11pm*
4) Nakau (なか卯) - gyudon and curry. *Bowls from 290 yen. • 24h*
5) Tenya (天丼てんや) - tempura. *Bowls from 500 yen • 11am-11pm*
6) Wendy's First Kitchen (ファーストキッチン) - cheap soups, burgers and pasta. *Pasta from 580 yen, burgers from 370 yen • 7am-11pm*
7) Hokka Hokka Tei (ほっかほっか亭) - bento boxes. *Bentos from 399 yen • 9:30am-9:30pm*

Local budget food

8) Kougaryu (甲賀流) - Popular Takoyaki (octopus balls) takeout in Amemura. *Takoyaki from 400 yen • 10am-8:30pm*
9) Takoyaki Wanaka (わなか) - Another popular Takoyaki chain in Osaka, in a few locations (see map). *Takoyaki from 400 yen • 10am-10pm*

Cheap supermarkets (スーパー)

If you don't have much time, Seijo Ishii (成城石井) has a branch in Namba station, but prices are a little high (10am-10pm). Better is Life (ライフ), near exit 30 of JR Namba station (9am-12am). There is also a 24 hour Foodium (foodium 東心斎橋) supermarket to the east of Shinsaibashi.

Shopping

Uniqlo (ユニクロ)

There are many branches of the budget clothes chain in Namba, the biggest being near Shinsaibashi subway station (11am-9pm).

Tokyu Hands (東急ハンズ)

Full of crazy, strange Japanese goods for you to laugh at and enjoy. Back scratchers, weird massage chairs, crazy robot toys and some unimaginable goods. Great for souvenirs and any novelties you want to take home. *10am-9pm • Near Shinsaibashi subway station*

Don Quijote (ドン・キホーテ)

There are two of these variety megastores on Dotonbori Street, full of all sorts of crazy, and sometimes super useful goods. *24h • Dotonbori Street*

3 Coins

300 yen shop, with higher quality, longer-lasting products than the 100 yen stores. Also has more fashion items, such as a good selection of accessories. *10am-9pm • Namba Town (なんなんタウン), the underground shopping mall between Nankai Namba station and Marui department store*

100 yen shops

Can Do (キャンドゥイ) - Inside Bic Camera. *10am-9pm*
Seria (セリア) - Near Amemura. *11am-9am*
Daiso (ダイソー) - One in Shinsaibashi (10am-9pm), and another in Namba station (10am-11pm).

Pharmacy (ドラッグストア)

Daikoku (ダイコク) also has a 100 yen store inside (8am-10:30).

How to get there and away

Namba is a bit of a maze, but most people will arrive via JR Namba station if using JR trains, Namba or Nippombashi stations if on the Osaka Subway, or Nankai Namba if using the Namba lines (such as from/to Koyasan). Some highway buses may also drop you off here. *Recommended rail passes: Enjoy Eco Card, Osaka Visitors' Ticket, Osaka Amazing Pass*

Tourist information (観光案内所)

Inside Nankai Namba station (9am-8pm).

Shinsekai (新世界)

It's amazing that places like this still exist. Shinsekai started to really make a name for itself after World War Two, when workers would come here after helping to rebuild the city for some drinks, casual food and maybe a bit of naughtiness! Many of these tightly packed establishments remain the same as they were just after the war, so it's a great area for a random walk around. It's one of Osaka's most interesting neighborhoods and a perfect spot for people watching and photo taking, both of which are free!

Things to do

Don Quijote (ドン・キホーテ)

This extra-large 'Mega' Don Quijote is full of interesting variety goods. Tax-free shopping is available on most items, such as on cosmetics, cheap food, alcohol and already bargain basement priced clothing. *9am-5am • Dobutsuen-Mae station exit 5, east of Shin-Imamiya station*

Daiso (ダイソー)

Another larger than normal branch of a budget chain store, this 100 yen shop has a pretty amazing selection. *9am-5am • Opposite Don Quijote*

Jan-Jan Lane (じゃんじゃん)

The main entertainment and restaurant street in Shinsekai. It still has many pubs and very unpretentious eating joints. The name comes from the strumming sound of a Japanese banjo, which was used by waitresses to attract customers into their establishment. *Head past Don Quijote, then past Daiso and take the first right. Jan-Jan is the second street on the left*

Tsutenkaku Tower (通天閣)

This very retro tower may be dwarfed by the SkyTower in Tokyo, but at 130 meters tall and based on the Eiffel Tower, it has become a symbol of Osaka. Most budget travelers tend to just hang around the area though. *Adults 600 yen, children 300 yen • 9am-9pm (last entry 8:30pm) • Top of Jan-Jan Lane*

Budget food

Budget restaurants

Hokka Hokka Tei (ほっかほっか亭) - Bento boxes. *Bentos from 399 yen • 10am-11pm • Opposite Don Quijote*
Matsuya (松屋) - Rice bowls and curry. *Gyudon bowls from 290 yen • 24h • Outside Ebisucho station (exit 4) to the north side*

Local budget food: Kushikatsu

Japanese shish kebab, known as Kushikatsu, is a fun activity. It is essentially skewered meats and vegetables, and patrons get to deep-fry the cutlets on their tables. Our local friends recommend Kushikatsu-Janjan (串かつじゃんじゃん) for those on a budget, but there are many around Shinsekai, so look around for any special offers. Also check the website at http://www.kushikatu-janjan.com/campaign/ for discount coupons (use Google Translate if you can't read Japanese). *Sticks from 80 yen • 11am-10:30pm • Halfway up Jan-Jan Lane, on right side*

Cheap supermarkets (スーパー)

Don Quijote has a large groceries section.

How to get there and away

Shinsekai is accessible via Dobutsuen-Mae on the subway or Shin-Imamiya on the JR and Nankai lines. It's also a 20-minute walk from Namba. Just head to Den Den Town, to the east of Namba station, then walk 15 minutes south down the main road. Shinsekai is just past Ebisucho subway station. *Recommended rail passes: Enjoy Eco Card, Osaka Visitors' Ticket, Osaka Amazing Pass*

Tourist information (観光案内所)

Nearest official tourist information center is in Namba.

Minoo Park (箕面公園)

One of Osaka's oldest parks, Minoo is a popular day trip from Osaka city, and a great place to go hiking away from all the skyscrapers and shopping malls. A perfect choice for a first-time hike in Japan, it's a very accessible and inexpensive to access hiking area, with options to expand your hike if you need something more challenging. Deep fried momiji leaves are the famous snack to try as you walk up.

Main hike up to waterfall

Most people take the main route up to the waterfall, which has a few detours if you have time. English language signs and maps along the way make it a breeze to add these on as you go. The waterfall is a worthwhile payoff for the walk up, at 33 meters tall and five meters wide. The pristine, quiet surroundings have understandably become a hotspot for meditation. Along the way there are also a few free temples, so pop into a few if you need a rest. In autumn the path is even more stunning, being lined with thousands of red and golden leaves. *Difficulty: Easy • Hike time: 2 hours*

Minoh Hotel

The free footbath near Minoh Hotel on the way up or down is a nice place to soothe your feet. You can also enter the hot spring for 1000 yen (4pm-12am). While not as pretty as some hot springs on the inside, the view from the outside bath is spectacular and there is a good variety of baths. There are also free retro video games to play and some cheap amusements.

Budget food

Momiji Street is where most of the action is. Look for "もみじ Street" to the hard right of the station. There are a few budget eat-in options here, but it's best to head to a convenience store. There is a 24 hour Daily Yamasaki convenience store outside the station, to the right. Head into the city for more cheap options in the evening.

100 yen shops
Daiso (ダイソー) - Head 10 minutes down Momiji Street. *10am-7pm*

Cheap supermarkets (スーパー)
The closest to the station is Sundi Supermarket (サンディ), which is three minutes down after taking the first left on Momiji Street.

How to get there and away

From Umeda station in central Osaka, take the Hankyu Takarazuka Line to Ishibashi station, then take the Hankyu Minoh Line to Minoh station (25 mins, 270 yen). Note that it's sometimes spelt Minoh.

Tourist information (観光案内所)

At the Minoo station building, with some good maps to take for free (9am-5pm).

Osaka Aquarium Kaiyukan (海遊館)

Generally considered to be the best aquarium in Japan, this gigantic structure houses more than 30,000 creatures from around 600 species, including favorites like penguins, sea lions, dolphins and sharks. Within the aquarium the natural habitats have been painstakingly recreated in the 15-plus mega tanks, with each one based on a region of the Pacific Rim. Interactive features include touching the fish (including sharks!), plus there are feeding shows throughout the day. *Adults 2300 yen, children 7-15 years 1200 yen, children 4-6 years 600 yen, under 4 years FREE • 10am-8pm • Osakako station on the Subway Chuo Line. From Umeda or Namba, take the Subway Midosuji Line to Hommachi, then the Chuo Line to Osakako (20 mins, 280 yen) •* http://www.kaiyukan.com/

Discount pass: Osaka Kaiyu Ticket

If as a budget traveler you are a bit shocked at the entrance fee, consider this pass. It includes access to the aquarium, plus unlimited use of subway, buses and the New Tram Line in Osaka city for one day. Also includes discounts of up to 50% for 30 other tourist sites in Osaka Bay. As the Osaka Kaiyu Ticket price is only a little more than a general admission ticket, this is a must purchase if your day's focus is the aquarium. *Adults 2550 yen, children 1300 yen • Sold at all subway and New Tram stations, plus tourist information centers. Not sold at the aquarium.*

Sumiyoshi Taisha Shrine (住吉大社)

In our opinion, if you are going to visit a shrine in Osaka, this is the one to go to. This shrine is the headquarters of more than 2000 Shinto shrines across Japan and is believed to enshrine three Shinto gods, one for protecting the nation, another for sea voyages and a third for waka (31-syllable) poetry. Registered as a national treasure, it also has a few unique aspects to it. The most interesting was watching Japanese people searching for special stones in a kind of spiritual game, with the aim seemingly to collect together three that have matching Japanese characters on them. It's on the way from the airport, so worth checking on the way in our out to save a buck on transportation. *FREE • 6:30am-5pm • From Namba station, take the Nankai Main Line to Sumiyoshi Taisha station (9 mins, 210 yen). Also on the Hankaidenki-Hankai Line • Recommended rail pass: Osaka Amazing Pass*

Umeda (梅田)

Originally an agricultural area when one of the first stations in Kansai was built here, Umeda has grown to become the business and shopping center of northern Osaka city. These days it's mainly expensive department stores, of which there are several dotted around Umeda and Osaka station offering tax-free shopping.

Things to do

Yawaragi-no-niwa Garden
Meaning "Peaceful Garden", Yawaragi-no-niwa is a stylish open space with a traditional Japanese rock and moss garden, right up on the 10th floor! Above there are some nice benches and tables, so bring a few drinks in the evening and watch over the city from above. *FREE • 7am-11pm • 10th and 11th floor of North Gate Building, connected to Osaka station*

Tenku-no-noen Farm
A farm on top of a skyscraper? Yes, that's right! This is a small rooftop farm, growing traditional vegetables from the local region, as well as herbs and fruits. There is even a tiny vineyard as well. Visitors can occasionally have a bit of fun helping out on the farm. *FREE • 7am-9pm • Via the stairs from Yawaragi-no-niwa Garden*

OPA (梅田ＯＰＡ店)

This shopping mall has a good selection of budget shops, such as ABC Mart for shoes, Daiso for 100 yen items and Thank You Mart for 390 yen goods. There is also a huge new Uniqlo and QU budget clothes store next door. Tax-free shopping available. *11am-9pm • Just east of Hankyu Umeda station (signs may point to ABC Mart)*

Budget food

While there are no real budget supermarkets around, there are some small, if a little pricey, food stores and plenty of large convenience stores in the station complexes. Be sure to head underground, as many of them are down there. Note that restaurants in the department stores are very expensive, but it's always worth checking out the food courts for any free samples to try out!

Head to Shin-Umeda Shokudogai, the underground mall near Subway Umeda station, and HEP FIVE department store, nearby on the east side, for budget options:

First Kitchen (ファーストキッチン) - Cheap soups, burgers and pasta. *Pasta from 580 yen, burgers from 370 yen • 7am-11pm • HEP FIVE*

Yoshinoya (吉野家) - Gyudon and curry. *Bowls from 330 yen • 6am-11:30pm • Shin-Umeda Shokudogai*

Sukiya (すき家) - Gyudon and curry. *Bowls from 360 yen • 24h • Behind the OPA shopping mall*

How to get there and away

The area can be reached via Osaka station if on a JR line, or Umeda station if using the subway, Hankyu or Hanshin lines. If on the subway Tanimachi Line, you can get off at Higashi-Osaka. *Recommended rail passes: Enjoy Eco Card, Osaka Visitors' Ticket, Osaka Amazing Pass*

Tourist information (観光案内所)

Hankyu Tourist Center is located in the Hankyu section of Umeda station (8am-5pm).

Osaka Castle (大阪城)

While this may not be the most authentic of castles in Japan (it does feature elevators!), Osaka castle is worth a visit if you have some time to kill or want to relax in its park, especially during the cherry blossom season. There are 13 structures within the castle's stone walls and moat, such as the Sengan Turret, classified an Important Cultural Property, and a museum. If you have already, or plan to visit another castle, skip the entrance fee here and just chill out in the park. *Adults 600 yen, children FREE • 9am-5pm • From Namba station, take the Subway Sennichimae Line to Tanimachi Kyuchome, then the Tanimachi Line to Tanimachi Yonchome station (10 mins, 230 yen). From Umeda/Osaka station, walk to Higashi-Umeda station, then take the Tanimachi Line to Tanimachi Yonchome station (6 mins, 230 yen) • Recommended rail passes: Enjoy Eco Card, Osaka Visitors' Ticket*

Around Kyoto and Osaka

Welcome to the west side. Kansai, the prefecture home to Kyoto and Osaka, has plenty of other great spots for budget travelers to explore. Highlights here are one of Japan's top three shrines in Ise, the spectacular Buddhist mountain retreat of Koyasan and the ever popular Nara, known for its deer feeding and huge temples. There are a large number of discount transportation passes covering the whole region, as well as some for specific tourist spots.

Discount passes

There are four really great passes in Kansai, so have a read through the guides in this chapter to see where you want to visit, then choose a pass if it's appropriate. Also consider the Kansai-Hiroshima Area Pass if you are visiting Hiroshima or Miyajima to the west as well.

JR Kansai Area Pass

Allows unlimited use of JR (national rail) trains, within the area stretching from Himeji in the west to Nara and Kyoto in the east. Use of Shinkansen is not permitted, but use of special rapid services, rapid services and local trains is. It covers all the cities in this chapter, with the exception of Koyasan (extra 830 yen from Hashimoto station in Wakayama) and Ise Grand Shrine (cheap buses from Kyoto and Osaka are available). The pass makes a lot of sense if you want to quickly travel to a new city every day. As an example, a one-way ticket from Himeji to Kyoto costs 2270 yen, meaning that visitors start to save money if they travel between quite distant cities each day. Otherwise, buying single tickets may actually be cheaper. Check your routes on Hyperdia to see if savings can be made. Only for those with tourist visas. Purchase online at http://www.westjr.co.jp/global/en/ticket/pass/kansai/, as prices increase slightly if purchasing in Japan. *1 day: Adults 2200 yen, children 1100 yen. 2 days: Adults 4300 yen, children 2150 yen. 3 days: Adults 5300 yen, children 2650 yen. 4 days: Adults 6300 yen, children 3150 yen.*

JR Kansai Wide Area Pass

For those who want to travel even further and faster in Kansai, check out the five-day Kansai Wide Area Pass. This also allows the use of the Shinkansen and limited express trains, and the pass extends further west to Okayama and Kurashiki, plus to northern cities in Kansai. If you want to speed up your journeys with the Shinkansen, this pass really starts to pay for itself. For example, a one-way Shinkansen ticket from Okayama to Kyoto costs 7100 yen, which is only 1900 yen short of the price for this five day pass. Only for those with tourist visas. Also purchasable online at http://www.westjr.co.jp/global/en/ticket/pass/kansai_wide/, with slightly higher prices if buying in Japan. *Adults 9000 yen, children 4500 yen*

Kansai Thru Pass

Allows unlimited use of non-JR train lines, from private networks such as Kintetsu, Hankyu, Nankai and Keihan. It also allows use of local transportation, such as the subways in Osaka and Kobe. Passengers can use the pass from the west in Himeji, south to Koyasan, and to the east to Kyoto, Uji, Osaka and Nara. Ise Grand Shrine still requires a bus or train from Kyoto or Osaka. If you want to include Koyasan, this pass will probably be better than the JR ones, plus it can also be used on non-consecutive days. Travel times will be longer with the Kansai Thru Pass, but the prices are much cheaper than the JR passes. The pass also includes more than 350 discounts at various shops, restaurants and tourist spots in the pass area, so you can save even more. For those with tourist visas only. Purchase at a ticket office of one of the train networks on the pass. *2 days: Adults 2000 yen, children 2000 yen. 3 days: Adults 5200 yen, children 2600 yen*

Kintetsu Rail Pass

Unlimited use of the Kintetsu Railway network for five days, which connects Osaka, Kyoto, Nara, Ise and Nagoya. A 'Plus' version also includes unlimited use of buses in Nara and Ise, with the extra cost of this pass being less than buying individual day passes in those cities. Does not include limited express trains, so journey times may be a little long. Unlike the other passes though, this one includes access to Ise Grand Shrine, so seriously consider it if going there. In addition to a host of discounts to shops, restaurants and tourist attractions, the Kintetsu Rail Pass also gives 6% (after getting your tax-free discount!) off at Bic Camera electronic shops in Osaka and Kyoto. Purchase from a travel agent abroad, as there are slight price increases if buying in Japan. *Normal pass: Adults 3600 yen, children 1800 yen. Plus pass: adults 4800 yen, children 2400 yen*

Sample itineraries

Kansai's best temples and shrines

Get yourself a Kintetsu Rail Pass for this one, and get the 'plus' version if you want to use the buses as well. Spend day one at Ise Grand Shrine for arguably Japan's best shrine, then head to Nara for a more varied selection of shrines and temple for day two and three. On day three, head to Kyoto when you are done with Nara, and continue into the fourth day, enjoying all the UNESCO World Heritage sites Kyoto has to offer. Kyoto has a huge selection, so on your last day stay here until you are ready to finish in Osaka.

Something a little different…

From Osaka, do a quick day trip up into the mountains in Koyasan. On day two, head to Uji, Kyoto's sometimes forgotten, but very rewarding, little brother. On the third day, either head west to see Himeji's new castle or chill out in funky Kobe. Perfect with the Kansai Thru Pass for three days.

Nara (奈良)

Nara is a large city full of UNESCO World Heritage shrines and temples, not far from Kyoto and Osaka. A must-visit for most foreign travelers coming to Japan, Nara has a large park where most of the action is, while there are a few more shrines and temples a short bicycle or bus ride away.

The ancient capital city of Japan from 710 to 794, during the Nara period, the city has had a strong Buddhist influence over the years. Since then Nara has been rather overshadowed by its big brothers in the Kansai region, however Nara is for many travelers more varied in its sights. The fact that most are quickly accessible from the train stations also makes it a great choice for budget travelers.

Discount pass: Nara Bus Pass

Not up for walking all day? With this pass visitors get unlimited use of Nara Kotsu buses, which can take visitors to all the main spots in Nara (wide pass also usable to outer temples such as Horinji Temple). Also includes discounts to 40 plus restaurants and shops, plus a handy map to make using the buses super easy. Pick up from a bus information center in JR Nara station or just outside Kintetsu Nara station. Note that if buying a Kintetsu Rail Pass, there are also '1-day', '2-day' and 'Plus' versions that include bus travel in Nara. *1 Day Pass 500 yen, 1 Day Wide Pass 1000 yen, 2 Day Pass 1500 yen (children half price)*

A little bit of history

Back in the 3rd century AD, the Yamato clan rose to power to become the original Japanese emperors, leading to the area being named the Yamato Plain. During the period up to the 7th century Japan had no permanent capital and usually the capital was moved when each emperor passed away, according to Shinto beliefs at the time. As Buddhism started to gain more popularity in Japan, this taboo started to become less important for the Japanese nobility and the practice died out when the entire country joined together under imperial control in 646.

Nara was selected as the capital, but this lasted for just 75 years due to the rather naughty priest named Dōkyō. He managed to seduce his way into taking over the throne, and the capital was moved away from Nara's powerful religious clans to Kyoto. While Nara was capital for only a short time, the influences of Chinese culture at the time had profound effects on Japanese arts and ways of life. The temples and shrines in Nara still remained powerful, giving the city the nickname "South Capital". It has left a surprisingly good number of mind-blowing shrines and temples for visitors to enjoy today.

Things to do

Nara Park Area (奈良公園)
Nara Park is well signposted and easy to get around.

Todaiji Temple (東大寺)
Founded all the way back in 728, this is Nara's main Buddhist temple and was once part of the 'Seven Great Temples', a once very powerful and influential group. Inside the complex the Great Buddha Hall features the world's largest bronze Buddha statue, known as Daibutsu. Inside there is a famous wooden column you can walk through for good luck and deer, regarded as messengers of god by the temples followers, roam the grounds. This UNESCO World Heritage site is a must-visit in Nara. Download the free 'Nara Audio Guide' before on your phone or tablet for the audio guide. *Adults 800 yen, children 400 yen • Open from 9:30am, closes 4:30pm (Nov - Feb), 5pm (Mar), 5:30pm (Apr - Sept), 5pm (Oct)*

Deer Spots
Say hello to the cute deer and feed them some biscuits if you or your children want to try it out. Just be careful of any deer that jump at you for food! Usually located in Nara Park and up towards Kasuga Taisha Shrine, difficult to miss. Biscuits for feeding from 150 yen.

Kasuga Taisha Shrine (春日大社)
The main Shinto shrine in Nara, famous for its bronze statues and eerie stone lanterns that lead up to the shrine. Just like the other World Heritage sites, Kasuga Taisha has a long and rich history, being founded in 768 AD. From 1871 to 1946 it was a Kanpei-taiha (1st rank shrine). Nearby is the Kasugayama Primeval Forest, a sacred area which is considered a good spot for a light hike or somewhere to relax for a while. The forest contains over 170 kinds of frees, 60 bird types and countless species of insects. Leave plenty of time to explore this fascinating, vast complex. *500 yen • Apr - Sept: 6:00-18:00, Oct - Mar: 6:30am-5pm*

Kofukuji Temple (興福寺)
Another of the eight World Heritage sites in Nara, this is a lovely temple complex right next to Kintetsu Nara station and one of the greatest temples from the 8th

century. Originally built in Kyoto, but moved to Nara when it became the capital in 710, Kofukuji features both a three-storey and five-storey pagoda (the second highest in Japan), an old bath house and a host of well looked after Buddhist structures. *Adults 600 yen, junior/high school children 500 yen, primary 200 yen • 9:00am-5pm*

Nara National Museum (奈良国立博物館)

Not an essential visit, but check this out if you want to know a little more about the area. Nara National Museum has a large selection of exhibits about the history and culture of Nara. Well stocked with Japanese paintings and writings, ancient bronzes, Buddhist sculptures and decorative arts. *Adults 520 yen, college students 260 yen, high school and below free. Free on May 5, May 18, third Monday of September, February 3 • Tues-Sun 9:30pm-5pm (open when Monday is national holiday, closed next day)*

Sarusawa Pond (猿沢池)

Relaxing pond on the way to the park, and a good place to chill out with some drinks or a bento box. Apparently it has some turtles, but we didn't see any!

Yoshikien Garden (吉城園)

The cheapest Japanese garden in Nara, as some of the others are crazily overpriced. Features a Japanese tea ceremony house, moss gardens and a pleasant pond. *250 yen (free for foreign tourists) • 9pm-5pm*

Mount Wakakusa (若草山)

342 meter high mountain to the east of Nara Park, giving an unobstructed view over the cities World Heritage listed shrines, temples and pagodas. The climb up is gentle, taking 40-50 minutes to reach the peak. Also a good place to visit during the cherry blossom season, when the mountain is full of sakura trees and visitors can see even more scattered over Nara. *150 yen • 9pm-5pm (closed mid-December to late March) • 10-minute walk past Todaiji and Kasuga Taisha*

West side

Heijo Palace (平城宮跡)

Previously the imperial residence when Nara was the capital. The grand palace and lawn were inspired by the Chinese city of Chang'an, which at the time was a prosperous powerhouse. Heijo Palace is therefore a worthwhile choice for those who may be a little tired of too many Japanese palaces or castles. The complex also features some interesting excavation grounds of the living quarters and ceremonial buildings. *Free (bring your passport, as museum is free for foreign visitors) • 9:00am-4:30pm • Take the train from Kintetsu Nara to Yamato-Saidaiji station (5 mins, 210 yen), then walk 5 mins (local buses also pass from JR Nara or Kintetsu Nara)*

Toshodaiji Temple (唐招提寺)

Founded as a place of training for Buddhists in the 7th century under the guidance of the Tang Dynasty in China and the first in Japan to be devoted to the Chinese Buddhist sect of Nanzan. Located in what used to be the center of capital Nara, Toshodaiji is considered to be a classical style of Buddhist temple. The main attraction is the recently renovated Golden Hall (kondō), a wide, tiled roofed building written about in many classical Japanese poems. *Adults 600 yen, junior/high school children 400 yen, primary 200 yen • 8:30am-5pm • From Kintetsu Nara, take a train via Yamato-Saidaiji to Nishinokyo (12 mins, 260 yen), then it's a 10 min walk. Buses no. 70, 72 and 97 from JR Nara and Kintetsu Nara (260 yen, 15 mins) also stop nearby*

Yakushiji Temple (薬師寺)

Build by Emperor Tenmu to cure the ills of his empress over 1000 years ago, with the original eastern pagoda still intact. One of the most famous imperial Buddhist temples, other buildings, monuments and pagodas have been faithfully reconstructed and well displayed. The prices are a little steep, so we would say this is skippable if you're running low on today's budget and are going to see other pagodas on your trip. *Adults 800 yen, junior/high school children 500 yen, primary 200 yen • 8:30am-5pm • From Kintetsu Nara, take a train via Yamato-Saidaiji to Nishinokyo (12 mins, 260 yen). Buses no. 70, 72 and 97 from JR Nara and Kintetsu Nara (260 yen, 15 mins) also stop nearby*

Cycle it!

The west side is a bit tricky to get too on bus, and spots are close enough to make individual bus rides troublesome and far enough from each other that walking can be too much for some. We recommend renting a bicycle and spend an afternoon around the west side temples.

Volunteer guides and tours

NPO Nara Guide - http://nara-guide-club.com/

Available in multiple languages, this group can take visitors to the main sites in and around Nara. Had the quickest responses to emails and super helpful.

Nara SGG Club - http://narakanko.jp/sgg/

The main volunteer club in Nara, they have 'model courses' to help you plan your visit. They can also get you in touch with other associated groups.

Nara Student Guide - http://www.narastudentguide.org/

Eager students from local universities can also take you around Nara. One-day tours of the major tourist areas and World Heritage sites offered.

Budget food

Around JR Nara

The JR station has a bunch of budget options, so consider picking something up from here for lunch or dinner if arriving at this station.

Matsuya (松屋) - Gyudon and burger eat-in and takeaway. *Meals from 290 yen • From JR Nara station east exit, walk past Super Hotel and then Lawson convenience store on your right, then take a right turn. Matsuya is a short walk down*

Honke-kamadoya Bento (本家かまどや) - Cheap bento takeaway shop. *Bento boxes from 300 yen • From JR Nara station, take a left at the information center and walk under the track. The bento shop is on the right a little down the street*

Yayoi Iken (やよい軒) - Reasonably priced Japanese teishoku (traditional set) meals. *Meals from 680 yen • Inside JR Nara station*

Around Kintetsu Nara and Nara Park

Head down Higashimuki and Sakura-dori for a host of options, including some convenience stores and a supermarket.

Sushi Maruchu (丸忠) - Take out sushi joint. *Sushi sets from 540 yen • In Kintetsu Nara station, on the concourse*

Sukiya (すき家) - Curry and gyudon eat-in and takeaway. *Meals from 360 yen • Just outside exit 5 of Kintetsu Nara station.*

West side

Heading towards the shrines on the west side there are a variety of cheap options for Japanese and western food in Ito Yokado shopping mall (イトーヨーカドー) and some road-side restaurants.

Yoshinoya (吉野家) - Gyudon eat-in and takeaway. *Meals from 330 yen • From JR Nara station East, take a walk to the left past the information center and KFC. Take a left at the main road, and Yoshinoya is just after going under the rail bridge.*

Kura Sushi (くら寿司) - Awesome 100 yen per plate sushi, worth visiting if you are heading to the west side. *1 plate from 108 yen • West of Kintetsu Nara station, just past Ito Yokado shopping mall (イトーヨーカドー), which is soon after you pass over the 2 narrow rivers.*

Hanamaru Udon (はなまるうどん) - Udon chain, popular with all ages for its varied menu. *Udon from 300 yen • Inside Ito Yokado mall (イトーヨーカドー).*

Shopping

Sanjo-dori Street

Nara's main shopping street, going all the way from JR Nara station to the park. A nice place to hang out, especially to pick up some touristy treats. Sanjo-dori has some large outlet shops and many antique stores. *From JR Nara station, take the east exit. Sanjo-dori is the street that goes under the track north of the tourist information center. Head opposite the rail bridge for most of the action.*

Higashimuki Shopping Arcade

A large variety of traditional Japanese goods and souvenirs. Prices can vary for shops and restaurants, so have a look around this busy area for the best deals. There is also a supermarket called Paket (パケット奈良店) at the entrance (8:30am-10pm). *From exit 2 of Kintetsu Nara station*

Mochiidono Shopping Arcade

Featuring a wide selection of ceramic, calligraphy, deer antler ornaments and other Nara specialty goods, this is Nara's top window-shopping street.
Next street down from Higashimuki arcade, after you meet up with Sanjo-dori

Naramachi Street

Traditional Japanese shopping street lined with merchant shops and warehouses from the old days. Loads of interesting shops and restaurants selling plenty of retro goods and meals. Best in the afternoon, when there is more of an atmosphere. *Walk down Sanjo-dori Street, then go down the road beginning with the Circle K convenience store (changing to a Family Mart after time of writing).*

100 yen shops
Seria (ビエラ) - In JR Nara station, 2nd floor. *10am-9pm*
Daiso (ダイソー) - From Kintetsu Nara station, take exit 4. Walk down Sakura Dori, take the first left. Walk down, then Daiso is just around the next corner, on the left. *10am-9pm*

Pharmacy (ドラッグストア)
Kintetsu Nara station has a Kokumin drug store (コクミンドラッグ), while the nearest to JR Nara is Daikoku drug store (ダイコクドラッグ), just up Sanjo-dori.

Recommended cheap accommodation

Hostels and guest houses

Guesthouse Naramachi
An old merchant's building with a very old-school atmosphere. Really helpful staff, cheap bike rental and inexpensive rooms. *Dorms from 2500, Japanese twin rooms from 7000 yen* • http://nara-naramachi.com/

Deer Guest House
Often recommended by readers, this hostel has a decent shared kitchen and free computers to use. *Right next to the park. Dorms from 2700 yen*

Hotel Pagoda
This hotel has some great budget options, especially for families and large groups. Located near Nara Park, this hotel also has traditional Japanese rooms. *Dorms from 3250 yen, doubles from 5000 yen, family rooms from 12000 yen*

Love hotels (adults only)

Hotel Chapel Classic
6-minute walk from JR Nara station, this love hotel has all the basic mod-cons and free parking. Rooms are minimalist, but sophisticated. Reservations possible on Booking.com. *Doubles from 3990 yen*

Internet cafes

Comic Buster Shalala (コミックバスター Shalala)
This well-known chain has two locations in Nara, for both the JR and Kintetsu stations. Free drinks bar available, plus private booths and vending machines for cheap food, but no showers. *Night packs (ナイトパック) available from 9pm: 6 hours (6 時間ナイトパック) 1600 yen, 9 hours (9 時間ナイトパック) 1900 yen, 12 hours (12 時間ナイトパック) 2400 yen*
JR Nara branch location: Take the east exit and walk up Sanjo-dori Street. Shalala is just past St. Marc Cafe (サンマルクカフェ) on the right (5th floor).
Kintetsu Nara branch location: Take exit 4, then walk left down Sakura Dori. Shalala is above Sun Drug (サンドラッグ), a few minutes down the street.

Getting around

Walking is the best way to get around Nara Park, near Kintetsu Nara station. Almost all bus stops in the city have buses going here. JR Nara station is located to the south west. Frequent bus services operate between these stations such as the 100 yen Nara Grutto buses (奈良公園ぐるっとバス), which has 2 loop courses (one for Nara Park, one for Heijo Palace).

How to get there and away

By rail

From Kyoto station, take the JR **Nara Line** to Nara (44 mins, 690 yen) or **Kintetsu/Kashihara** Line to Kintetsu Nara (1 hour, 1130 yen). From Osaka, take the **Kintetsu Nara Line** from Osaka-Namba station (within Namba subway station) to Kintetsu Nara station (36 mins, 540 yen) or the JR Yamatoji Line from Osaka station to Nara (50 mins, 800 yen). *Usable rail passes: Japan Rail Pass, Kansai Area Pass, Kansai Wide Area Pass, Kansai-Hiroshima Area Pass, Kintetsu Rail Pass, Kansai Thru Pass*

By bus

From Tokyo or other major cities, get a bus with Willer Express or JR Bus (from 5980 yen, 7 hours). *Usable bus pass: Japan Bus Pass*

Tourist information (観光案内所)

Nara City Information Center is just outside the JR station, east exit. Kintetsu Nara Station Information Center is inside Kintetsu Nara station.

Kobe (神戸)

Kobe is a stylish city not far from Kyoto and Osaka, that is known as one of the first ports in Japan to open up to foreigners. Kobe was therefore the city that brought many international foods, drinks and sports to Japan. Most people tend to spend a day here on the way from Osaka to Hiroshima, and it's a great way to add a bit of variety to your trip. The main area is Sannomiya, which is the largest shopping area and best place to stay nearby. Along with the Kitano-cho area, Kobe is a good place to take a free stroll, meaning it can be a good spot for budget travelers.

Discount passes

Kobe Welcome Coupon

Special discounts and other benefits at more than 50 tourism spots, shops and restaurants in Kobe. Also includes some transportation discounts, such as on the City Loop bus and on the water shuttle to Kansai International Airport. Print it off online at http://plus.feel-kobe.jp/coupon/ and be sure to bring your passport when you use it. Also available at tourism information centers.

Discount pass: City Loop Bus 1-Day Pass

Unlimited use of the City Loop bus, which takes visitors to all the major spots, for just 660 yen (children 330 yen). Available at the tourist information centers or on the bus. A great choice if you don't want to be walking around all day. Also includes more than 30 discounts and benefits at some of the sightseeing areas.

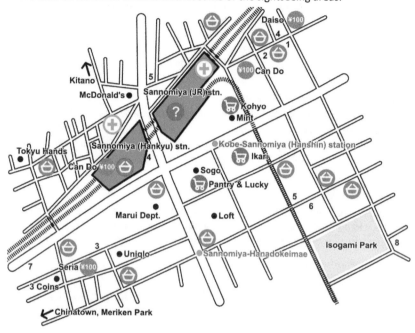

Things to do

Around Sannomiya

Chinatown (南京町)

One of Japan's top three Chinatowns, this is a great place for a nice walk-around. The grand Changan Gate sits at the eastern end, with the Xian Gate on the other side. In between there are lots of rather exotic Chinese goods on sale. It's a bit of tourist trap for prices, so best to eat dinner elsewhere. There are some small shops selling dumplings, Chinese sweets and toys though, so budget travelers may see the odd gem. *Near Motomachi station*

Meriken Park (メリケンパーク)

Great place to eat your cheap bento or have a beer in the evening. Full of all sorts of strange sculptures, architecture and some fancy powerboats on display. *FREE • 24h • 15-minute walk south of Chinatown*

Sorakuen Garden (相楽園)

Kobe's best traditional Japanese garden. The elegantly designed garden seems unchanged since it was built in 1885. Originally built for a wealthy merchant by the name of Taijiro Kodera, the splendid garden is now open for all to see. *Adults 300 yen, children 150 yen • 9am-5pm • Near Kenchō-mae station on the Kobe Subway*

Kitano-cho (北野)

This was the area where foreigners were first allowed to stay when Kobe opened up to them. Have a stroll around and you will see lots of nice European-style architecture, with countless old embassies, residences and new country-themed shops and amusements. Some are free to walk around, and we have found that, unless you are particularly interested in the country of the site, it's not really worth paying to go inside. *To access Kitano, take the loop bus or walk north from Sannomiya (15 minutes).*

Kitano Tenman Shrine (北野天満宮)

Provides amazing views over the city. The deity of study, Sugawara-no-Michizane, is enshrined at this temple. The main hall was constructed 260 years ago, and is surrounded by various officially designated cultural assets, such as a hall of worship and a torii gate. *FREE • 24h • Just north of the Kitano tourist information center, across the road*

Walk it and save!

If you like a bit of walking, then most of the main spots can be accessed on foot. For example, Kitano is a 15-minute walk from Sannomiya, while Chinatown is only 10 minutes away. Use the arrows on the Kobe map for directions.

Volunteer guides and tours

Kobe SGG club - http://www.kobesgg.org/

Focuses on the many sites around Kobe, plus specialist tours such as the sake and wine tour. Two weeks' notice required.

Kobe Voluntary Good-Will Guides (K.V.G.G) chiko-i-kvgg@kcc.zaq.ne.jp

Another good volunteer guide group, this one also ventures out to nearby towns and cities. At least a few days' notice required.

Budget food

Budget restaurants on map

1) Mos Burger (モス) - Japanese burgers. *Burgers from 220 yen • 7am-11pm*

2) Matsuya (松屋) - rice bowls and curry. *Gyudon bowls from 290 yen • 24h*

3) Ootoya (大戸屋) - Japanese set meals. *Sets from 750 yen • 11am-10pm*

4) Yoshinoya (吉野家) - gyudon and curry. *Bowls from 330 yen • 24h*

5) Nakau (なか卯) - gyudon and curry. *Bowls from 290 yen. • 24h*

6) Origin Bento (オリジン) - bento boxes. *Bentos from 390 yen • 7am-11pm*

7) Honke Kamadoya (本家かまどや) - bento boxes. *Bentos from 399 yen • 10am-8:30pm*

8) Hotto Motto (ほっともっと) - bento boxes. *Bentos from 390 yen • 10am-9:30pm*

Cheap supermarkets (スーパー)

Sogo Department Store has a Pantry & Lucky supermarket (そごうパントリー) in the basement floor (10am-8pm), and next door is Ikari (いかりスーパー), which has a good choice of foreign goods and drinks (10am-10pm). There is also a Kohyo (Peacock) supermarket, which has the MaxValu brand of cheap food and drinks, in the Mint Kobe (ミント神戸) department store (11am-9pm). All the above department stores are connected to the Hanshin Kobe-Sannomiya underground station.

Shopping

Uniqlo

Large branch of the best Japanese budget clothing brand. *11am-9am • South west of Sannomiya station*

3 Coins

Everything is 300 yen! Like the 100 yen shops, but better quality and more choice. *11am-9am • South west of Sannomiya station*

100 yen shops

Can Do (キャンドゥイ) - Two locations, one in the Daiei Kobe (Aeon) shopping mall (10am-9pm) and another in the Hankyu Sannomiya station building, on the north side near the Namco gaming arcade (11am-10pm).
Daiso (ダイソー) - This larger 100 yen shop is just down the road from the above Daiei Kobe, in Hankyu Oasis department store. *9am-10pm*
Seria (セリア) - Inside the shopping arcade near Uniqlo. *10am-9pm*

Pharmacy (ドラッグストア)

The easiest to locate is the Kokumin pharmacy (コクミンドラッグ) at the east exit of JR Sannomiya.

Recommended cheap accommodation

Hostels and guest houses

Yume Nomad
A cool guesthouse with nice communal areas to meet people and get some good travel advice. Also has bicycle rentals for a small fee. *Dorm beds from 2100 yen*

Kobe Sannomiya R2 Hostel
Friendly hostel with a good kitchen, plus free coffee and tea. Various types of rooms available, including some with dividers between the beds for more privacy and a better night's sleep. *Dorm beds from 2600 yen*

Capsule hotels

Capsule Hotel Kobe Sannomiya
Near to the station, this capsule hotel also has public baths and a sauna included. *Capsules from 2800 yen*

How to get there and away

By rail
Shin-Kobe is on the Shinkansen line, with frequent services. Shin-Kobe is 12 minutes from Shin-Osaka, 28 mins from Kyoto and about 3 hours from Tokyo. For those without a rail pass coming from the east, first make your way to Osaka, then take the JR Special Rapid to Sannomiya station (22 mins, 390 yen). *Recommended rail passes: Japan Rail Pass, Kansai Thru Pass, Kansai Area Pass, Kansai Wide Area Pass, Kansai-Hiroshima Area*

By bus
From Tokyo or other major cities, get a bus with Willer Express or JR Bus (from 4590 yen, 9 hours). *Recommended bus pass: Japan Bus Pass*

Tourist information (観光案内所)

The Kobe Information Center is located on the south side of JR Sannomiya station (9am-7pm). There is also an information center in Kitano, near Kitano Tenman-Jinja (9am-6pm, until 5pm Nov-Feb).

Uji (宇治)

Byodoin Temple

Uji is a well-known day trip from Osaka, Nara or Kyoto, famous across Japan for its high quality matcha tea production, and now across the world for its two UNESCO World Heritage sites. Over the centuries its location allowed Uji to blossom as a crossroad connecting Nara and Kyoto. Uji has also been blessed with amazing nature and is a good place to come for a light walk or hike. There is therefore lots to do for budget travelers, and it's very easy to fill up a day without spending too much.

Discount passes

If coming from Osaka or Kyoto, then a Sightseeing Pass from Keihan Railway may save you a bit. These two passes allow unlimited use of the Keihan lines for one or two days, and also include coupons for more than 20 locations. The wider area pass may really make sense for you if doing Uji as detour between Osaka and Kyoto. If just doing a day trip from Kyoto station, it's a little cheaper to just take the JR train without a pass. Get at Keihan stations. *Kyoto + Uji area: Adults 500 yen, children 250 yen (1 day). Osaka, Kyoto and Uji area: Adults 700 yen, children 350 yen (1 day), Adults 1,000 yen, children 500 yen (2 day)*

Things to do

Walk it and save!

The area is all super walkable, another plus for budget travelers. All the below sites are well signposted and easy to access from the stations.

Byodoin Temple (平等院)

Set on the west bank of Uji River, it's hard to imagine that this spectacular temple used to be a villa of the powerful lord Fujiwara-no-Yorimichi. The main temple structure will really take your breath away, and it's soon understandable how it became a UNESCO World Heritage site. Converted into a temple in the 17th century, it's said to have been designed to create a kind of paradise for the noblemen of the time. A stunning example of Buddhist architecture and gardening, this temple also features a great modern treasure museum. *Adults 300 yen, children 100 yen • 9am-5pm*

Byodoin Omotesando (平等院表参道)

The main shopping street to Byodoin Temple is a good place to try the hugely popular Uji green tea, especially as many shops are giving out free tea to try! All sorts of variations are on offer, from ice cream to biscuits to matcha drinks.

Uji River and Kisen Bridge (喜撰橋)

Head over Kisen Bridge, a large traditional red bridge, to enter a small island containing a few pieces of Japanese architecture and some statues to admire. The walk there is actually more interesting though, lined with tiny shops and warehouses that look like they came straight from the Edo period. Also provides a nice view of the surrounding mountains. *FREE • 24h • Just to the east of Byodoin Temple*

Koshoji Temple (興聖寺)

A quiet temple that is especially great during autumn colors. Has some unique and striking garden features that make it a must visit, it's a real surprise that so few people venture up to see it. *FREE • 9am-5pm • Head down south on the north side of Uji River, then take the 3rd left after the red bridge (through the small temple gate and up)*

Daikichiyamafuchi Park Hike (大吉山 風致公園)

A short 30 minute hike up the hill that gives a great view over Uji. Moderately steep at some points, but away from all the crowds on most days. *Take a right turn just before entering the Koshoji Temple grounds and walk up. After a few minutes take a right, then take a left up the hike path. Continue up the hill and down to Ujigami Shrine*

Ujigami Shrine (宇治上神社)

Sadly overlooked by the many who head straight to Byodoin Temple and the matcha tea shops, Ujigami Shrine is also a very significant sight, as it is believed to be the oldest shrine in Japan. The inner shrine has been designated a national treasure and is the second UNESCO World Heritage site in Uji. This shrine is built in a classic, minimalist Shinto style and packed into a small alcove, surrounded by quiet nature. *FREE • 9am-4:30pm*

Sawarabi Road Walk

After visiting Ujigami Shrine, we recommend heading down to the main bridge via Uji Shrine (宇治神社). It makes for a relaxing stroll past some interesting old-style homes and cafes.

Budget food

Eating out options are limited for budget travelers as this is quite a touristy area. Head to the supermarket or a convenience store for lunch, or to one of these:
Hokka Hokka Tei (ほっかほっか亭) - Bento boxes. *Bentos from 399 yen • 9:30am-9:30pm • JR Uji south exit, opposite 7-Eleven.*
Hakodate Ichiba (函館市場) - Conveyer belt sushi. *Sushi from 120 yen • 11:30-10pm • Near Keihan Uji station.*

Cheap supermarkets (スーパー)

The best supermarket is Happy Terada (ハッピーテラダ), which has a large stock of cheap food and drinks (10am-8pm). First head to JR Uji station, then walk down the stairs on the left from the north exit. Walk down the narrow road, take a left turn and the supermarket is a minute down, near the tracks.

How to get there and away

From JR Kyoto station, take the **Nara Line** to Uji (30 mins, 240 yen). If using one of the above Keihan passes, from Kyoto take a train from Gion Shijo station (30 mins) or from Osaka take a train from Kyobashi (50 mins). From Nara station, take the **Nara Line** to Uji (40 mins, 500 yen). *Usable rail passes: Japan Rail Pass, Kansai Area Pass, Kansai Wide Area Pass, Kansai-Hiroshima Area Pass, Kansai Thru Pass*

Tourist information (観光案内所)

Just outside JR Uji station, south exit (9am-5pm).

Ise Grand Shrine (伊勢神宮)

As one of the official top three shrine areas in Japan, Ise Grand Shrine is well worth the journey. The simple, yet spectacular shrines really have to be seen with your own eyes. One third of the town's land is owned by the 2000-years-old institution, which has kept it mainly forested. The town is considered to be Japan's religious and spiritual center.

Discount pass: Ise Toba Michikusa Kippu

Unlimited use of the loop buses connecting all the main spots, plus 10 to 20% discounts on entrance fees for several tourist attractions. Worth it if you are going to travel a few times on the bus, otherwise just get single tickets. Buy at Sanco Bus ticket booths in the station or at the tourist information center. *Adults 1000 yen, children 500 yen*

Things to do

Ise Shopping Street

Just outside Iseshi station, you will pass this street on the way to Ise Shrine Geku. It's full of interesting shops, making for a good hour or two of window shopping. As ever, be sure to pop in even if it seems over your budget, as free samples may be on offer!

Outer Shrine (Geku) (伊勢神宮外宮)

The outer shrine, also known as the Grand Shrine, is the real chart topper here. A stunning piece of minimalist architecture, it enshrines Toyouke Omikami, the Shinto deity and guardian of food, housing and clothing. Back in the Edo period, a once-in-a-lifetime pilgrimage to the Grand Shrine was considered a way to achieve true religious purification. The site, more than 1500 years old, is bustling with tourists and worshippers, but the huge size of the place stops it from feeling too crowded. *FREE • 5am-5pm • Head down the shopping street from Iseshi station*

Inner Shrine (Naiku) (伊勢神宮内宮)
A large collection of little shrines, plus the big new one, it enshrines the sun goddess Amaterasu Omikami, the mythological ancestor of the Imperial Family. It's considered the holiest site in the whole of Japan for many Japanese and to be a "power spot" for spiritual energy. Believed to have been established more than 2000 years ago, its buildings almost resemble rice granaries, owing to the fact they were first built before the introduction of Buddhist architecture from mainland Asia. *FREE • 5am-5pm • On CAN-Bus and the Geku-Naiku Loop Line buses*

Oharaimachi (おはらい町)
800 meter stone paved shopping street, full of traditional wooden built souvenir shops. Make sure you try Ise miso noodles, the famous dish in Ise, with prices ranging from 650 to 800 yen. The extra-thick and soft udon noodles are dipped in a dark broth made of tamari shoyu (soy sauce), and it's available from various shops and restaurants along the street. *Starts near entrance to Ise Grand Shrine*

Walk it and save!
It would be possible to walk from the Outer Shrine (Geku) to the Inner Shrine (Naiku). It takes about an hour, south down Route 32, which is the main road outside the Outer Shrine. It would also be possible to walk south down the Kintetsu Line, via Isuzugawa station. The places along the way aren't of great interest, but it's a nice way to see everyday life in the city.

Getting around
CAN-Bus and the Geku-Naiku Loop Line buses run frequently to all the main spots, if you don't want to walk all the way (430 yen from Ise Shrine Geku to Ise Grand Shrine).

Budget food
Budget travelers should use the convenience stores (a few around the stations) or the supermarket listed below for food in Ise. The Ise Miso Noodles are worth trying in Oharaimachi though.

Cheap supermarkets (スーパー)
Gyutora Supermarket (ぎゅーとら) is located a few minutes down to the right from Kintetsu Iseshi station, exit 2 (9am-10pm).

Recommended cheap accommodation

Kazami Guest House
A well regarded hostel with cheap rates, based in an old building with lots of charm. *Dorms from 2600 yen •* http://ise-guesthouse.com/en/

Yumebito House
A short walk from the station and with super low prices. Good recreation lounge to hang out in and meet some fellow travelers. *Dorms from 2300 yen*

How to get there and away

By rail

From Tokyo, first head to Nagoya. From Nagoya station, take the **Kintetsu Nagoya Line** to Iseshi station (2 hours, 1410 yen). The faster limited express is covered by the Kintetsu Rail Pass. From Osaka, first go to Tsuruhashi station (Sennichimae Line), then take the Kintetsu Osaka Line to Iseshi station (2 hours, 1750 yen). There is also a JR station. *Recommended rail passes: Kintetsu Rail Pass, Japan Rail Pass*

By bus

Willer Bus has buses to/from Tokyo (9 hours, from 3500 yen), while bus companies such as Mie Kostu Bus have cheap buses to/from Osaka (3 hours, from 1250 yen) and Kyoto (3.5 hours, from 1250 yen). Bookings can be made at the tourist information center in Ise, the bus terminals in Osaka and Kyoto, or Shinjuku Bus Terminal. *Recommended bus pass: Japan Bus Pass*

Tourist information (観光案内所)

Inside Iseshi station and in front of the Geku Shrine (9am-5:30pm).

Koyasan (高野山)

Koyasan is becoming increasingly popular as a side trip from Osaka, and is a perfect antidote to the downtown hustle and bustle of the big city. Located in the Koya-Ryujin Quasi-National Park, Koyasan will really take your breath away. The UNESCO World Heritage site has the head temple and sites of Esoteric Buddhism, up on the peak of a mysterious mountain. The temples will stun you with their beauty and size. There are dozens of temples in the area, plus ruins to explore along some well signposted hiking routes. All in all, a great spot for budget travelers.

Travel discounts and packages

Koyasan World Heritage Ticket

Cheapest and easiest way to visit the UNESCO World Heritage site of Koyasan if you want to stay a night there. It provides a return ticket on the **Nankai Line**, use of the cable car, and unlimited use of local Nankai Rinkan buses. It also comes with 20% off discount coupons for admission to many of the areas sites. For those looking to buy souvenirs, pass holders get 10% off at a few shops in town. Definitely worth it, as a regular full return fare is 2520 yen, and you will probably want to use the bus multiple times. Buy at Nankai Namba station. *Two day pass 3400 yen*

World Heritage Koyasan One-Day Free Ticket

A great option if you are only going for a day, this ticket allows unlimited use of buses in Koyasan, plus the above discounts and more. It doesn't include the train and cable car to Koyasan, but saves you a little and gives more flexibility with transportation to/away from Koyasan, especially if you plan to use the hiking routes to skip the cable car and/or train. Also a good option if you are using a national or regional train pass to get here, and want a day pass just for the local buses. Buy from the bus office in front of Koyasan station. *Adults 830 yen, children 420 yen*

Things to do

Kongobuji Temple (金剛峯寺)

The HQ for the local Buddhist sect, which now has more than 4000 temples across Japan. Features a great collection of traditional shoji screen paintings, religious artifacts and carvings, plus a Japanese rock garden. Built by the monk Kobo Daishi in the 9th century, it's the oldest building on the mountain. After he built it on the mountain, many other monks started to gather here and used it as the main site to study Buddhism. The quiet mountains of Koyasan provided a perfect spot to do this, and the whole mountain became a site of worship. *Adults 500 yen, children 200 yen • 8:30am-5pm • Kongobuji-mae bus stop*

Okunoin Temple and Graveyard (奥の院)

A truly fascinating graveyard, any time of the year. There are a host of statues, famous gravestones and a peaceful river flowing through. The golden temple at the end, surrounded by the forest, is a wonderful site and worth the walk up. *FREE • 24h • Okunoin-Mae bus stop*

Konpon Daito Temple (根本大塔)

A huge red temple with a towering pagoda. Enter at the front to check out the gold statues inside, and listen to the traditional Buddhist bells chime in the breezy winds. *200 yen • 8:30am-5pm • Daito-mae or Kondo-mae bus stops*

Kondo Hall (金堂)

Worth a quick visit, as it provides a nice contrast to the other buildings in the area. Interesting Buddhist statues and ornaments inside. *200 yen • 8:30am-5pm • Next to Konpon Daito Temple*

Reihokan Museum (霊宝館)

The main museum in Koyasan, visitors can explore a good selection of beautiful Buddhist paintings, ornaments and treasures from around Koyasan. The shape is said to resemble the Byodoin in Uji. *Adults 600 yen, children 350 yen • 8:30am-5pm • Daito-mae or Kondo-mae bus stops*

Daimon Gate (大門)

This grand 25 meter high Buddhist gate is the entrance to the town, and built to protect it from evil spirits. Also a good spot to start a hike. *FREE • 24h • Daimon bus stop*

Tokugawa Clan Mausoleum (徳川家霊台)

Built in 1643 by the Tokugawa shogun and his family, the structure took 20 years to bring to completion. The outside is constructed of unfinished wood, while the interior is decorated in gold leaf. There is a small collection of golden Buddhist ornaments inside. *200 yen • 8:30am-5pm • Namikiri-Fudo-mae bus stop*

Hiking in Koyasan

Before starting any of these hikes, it's recommended to check the latest track conditions and any route changes at the tourist information center in Koyasan or at Nankai Namba station. Bus stops are at all the starting and end points.

Fudozaka Route

Starting at Koyasan station (last stop on the train), this route goes via Gokuraku Bridge and up the mountain to Fudozaka-guchi Nyonindo (which is another 30 mins walk from the town). It's a good way to skip on the price of the cable car, or just a great hike that is not too taxing. Do it in reverse if you are not into hiking up. *Difficulty: Easy • Hike time: 1 hour*

Koyasan Women Pilgrims Route

Starts from the top of the Fudozaka Route (Fudozaka-guchi Nyonindo) and heads around the mountain to Okunoin. Note that you can also join the route from Daimon (entrance from behind Daimon), but be careful that you are going down the right route. Several interesting ruins dot the route, plus there is some stunning nature along the way. *Difficulty: Easy • Hike time: 2.5 hours*

Koyasan Sanzan Route

This route heads more out into the mountains, so is steeper but more out into nature and away from the crowds. This grand course goes all the way from Fudozaka-guchi Nyonindo to Okunoin, so it's possible to combine this route with others if you want a more challenging hike. *Difficulty: Medium • Hike time: 3 hours*

Volunteer guides and tours

Wakayama Volunteer Club - http://www.geocities.jp/wivcinfo/

Very responsive and organized volunteer group, which can take visitors around the main sites in Koyasan, as well as other spots in the prefecture. They do ask for 4000 yen, but this includes transportation costs. Apply at least two weeks in advance.

Getting around

There is a good, easy to understand bus network, use of which is included with the Koyasan passes. It's also possible to walk everywhere (apart from the bus-only road from the cable car station to town), with Daimon to Okunoin being only about 3km.

Budget food

There are no budget chain restaurants in Koyasan, but there are a few traditional family-run joints, offering the usual selection of noodles, curry and Japanese set meals (located near the Tourism Information Center and Senjuin-Bashi bus stop). Expect to pay more than you would in the cities, from 800-900 per meal, and note some close in the evenings. Especially if you are staying at Koyasan Guest House Kokuu, bring your food from a supermarket in Osaka and use the kitchen facilities at your accommodation. As it can be chilly, bring some Cup Noodles!

Cheap supermarkets (スーパー)

While there is no large supermarket here, Koyasan has a convenience store called New Yamasaki (ニューヤマザキデイリーストア), formally named Coco. Head down the side street at the post office (near the tourist information center), take the first left and walk down a minute or two.

Recommended cheap accommodation

Many visitors to Koyasan stay in one of the Buddhist temples, but the prices are way too high for most budget travelers. Book the following hostel ASAP, as at time of going to press there are no other budget options:

Koyasan Guest House Kokuu
While not temple lodgings, it's by far the cheapest place in Koyasan. In a good location, near a bus stop, with clean rooms, free wifi and kitchen facilities to cook in the hostel. *Capsule style beds from 3500 yen* • http://koyasanguesthouse.com/en/

How to get there and away

From Nankai Namba station (next to Namba subway station), take the Nankai Koya Line to Gokurakubashi (90 mins, 870 yen without a pass). You may need to change at Hashimoto. If the train is going direct to Gokurakubashi, make sure you are in the front carriage, as the train splits at Hashimoto. Once at Gokurakubashi station take the cable car to the top. From there a bus will be waiting to take you into Koyasan town center. There is also a hiking route from Koyasan station (see the Fudozaka Route) to/from Daimon, which may be of interest if you are just traveling with a backpack. This is also a nice way to save money if you don't have one of the passes. *Usable rail pass: Kansai Thru Pass*

Tourist information (観光案内所)

Near Senjuin-Bashi bus stop (8:30am-7pm Mar-Nov, 9am-5pm Dec-Feb).

West of Kyoto and Osaka

Itsukushima Shrine and Otorii Gate, Miyajima

Most first timers to Japan head all the way to Hiroshima and Miyajima on western Honshu. Visitors to Hiroshima can learn about the city's dark past and see the world famous floating Japanese gate on the coast of Miyajima. There are also some other great spots for newbies and regulars alike, such as the often forgotten mountain castle in Bitchu-Takahashi and the lovely traditional canal town of Kurashiki. For us though, the main highlight is the newly rebuilt Himeji Castle, Japan's most famous and deservedly a UNESCO World Heritage site.

Discount pass: Kansai-Hiroshima Area Pass

The Kansai-Hiroshima Area Pass allows unlimited travel on JR (national rail) trains for five days within Kansai and southern Chugoku, from Miyajima in the west to Nara in the east. As it allows for use of the Shinkansen in this area, it's a great way to see lots of western Honshu (Japan's main island) in a short amount of time. Even using highway buses and local trains would not be that much cheaper, and a Shinkansen ticket from Kyoto to Hiroshima is nearly as much as the cost of the pass. It provides access to nearly all the places in this guide in between (Bitchu-Takahashi and Koyasan need extra journeys). Get before coming to Japan. *Adults 13500 yen, children 6750 yen*

Sample itinerary: Western Honshu in five days
Spend day one in Kobe, a trendy city with a large Chinatown. Next, continue on to the World Heritage castle in Himeji. On day three, see one of Japan's best Japanese gardens in Okayama and the traditional city of Kurashiki. Spend the fourth day learning about Hiroshima, then enjoy a day of hiking on the stunning Miyajima island. Finally back on the Shinkansen to Osaka.

Hiroshima (広島)

An extremely emotional, often sad place, but it's one that must be visited. During World War II, a nuclear bomb destroyed Hiroshima and most places for tourists are related to this. One day is enough here, so most people head back to Osaka or Kyoto after visiting Hiroshima. As much of the spots are free, or almost free, it's also cheap to visit.

A little bit of history

While best known internationally for upsetting reasons, Hiroshima first began to prosper as a town towards the end of the 6th century. It was on the main transportation route along the south coast, which helped it to prosper. In 1589, a warlord by the name of Mori Terumoto built the castle and named the city Hiroshima. But hundreds of years later, in August 1945, the city was destroyed by an atomic bomb towards the end of World War Two. In later years the city made a surprisingly fast recovery and is now the economic and political capital of the region.

Discount pass: 1 Day Streetcar Pass

Allows unlimited use of trams in the Hiroshima area for one day. The main sites are quite far away from Hiroshima station, so it's recommended to get this pass and save a little if you don't want to walk too much. If you want to quickly do Miyajima as well then the ferry can also be added on to the pass, but it would really be pushing it to do it all in one day. Buy from the information desk in front of the Hiroshima station tram stop platform. *Adults 600 yen, children 300 yen (120 yen extra for Miyajima Ferry use)*

Walk it and save!

If you don't mind lots of walking, then rather than getting a tram pass you could attempt to walk everywhere. Follow the tram lines from Hiroshima station so you don't get lost. From Hiroshima station to the Atomic Dome takes 30 minutes along the tracks, then it's another 20 minutes north to the castle and then another 20 minutes east to the station. There are shopping streets along the way with lots of convenience stores, drug stores and more for cheap drinks and food. It's a pleasant way to see what a mid-sized Japanese city is like.

Things to do

Atomic Dome (原爆ドーム)

One of the few buildings in central Hiroshima to survive the atomic blast. The first atomic bomb used to attack a city was detonated only 160 meters southwest of the Atomic Dome, then the Hiroshima Prefectural Commercial Products Exhibition Hall. The atomic blast and heat wave completely gutted the building, but amazingly the main structure survived, even though all those inside instantly perished. A somber, but essential visit. *FREE • Genbaku Dome-mae tram stop*

Hiroshima Peace Memorial Park (平和記念公園)

Take some time out here to view the cenotaphs and monuments to those lost in the atomic blast, as well as those hoping for a nuclear-free future. Some stunning pieces of work. *FREE • 24h • Across bridge, to the south of Atomic Dome*

Hiroshima Peace Memorial Museum (広島平和記念資料館)

A must visit in Hiroshima, this museum is dedicated to eradicating nuclear weapons and aiming for world peace. A detailed account of what happened after the atomic blast is shown, including the effects of the atomic bomb exposure period. Old pictures, archived films and models help to explain the horrific experience that the city went through. Make sure you have plenty of time to explore this museum. *Adults 50 yen, children 30 yen • 8:30am-6pm • South side of Peace Memorial Park*

Hiroshima Castle (広島城)

A large castle with interesting castle grounds, the site was designated a National Treasure in 1931. Destroyed by the atomic bomb, it was later rebuilt and a history museum focusing on samurai culture was added. Highly recommended for cherry blossoms. *Adults 360 yen, children 180 yen • 9am-6pm (Mar - Nov), 9am-5pm (Dec - Feb) • 10-minute walk north of Kamiyacho-Nishi tram stop*

Shukkeien Garden (縮景園)

Created all the way back in the 16th century by a renowned tea ceremony master to serve as a villa and grounds for the feudal lords. Shukukeien Garden has a design that is said to condense the beauty of mountains, rivers and the feeling of Kyoto into one garden. A nice place for a stroll. *Adults 260 yen, children 150 yen • Apr - Sept: 9am-6pm, Oct - Mar: 9am-5pm • Shukkeien-Mae station*

Volunteer guides and tours

Hiroshima SGG club - taif@fureai-ch.ne.jp **or (082) 843-9030**
Meeting at Hiroshima station (or your hotel if requested), these English speaking guides can take you to the main spots in the city, as well as down to Miyajima. Contact at least 10 days in advance.

Budget food

Most people eat out in Hondori shopping street, which has loads of cool shops and restaurants, plus the usual selection of cheap chain eateries.

Budget restaurants

Ootoya (大戸屋) - Japanese set meals. *Sets from 750 yen • 10am-10pm • Down Hondori street and near McDonald's from Hondori tram stop*
Yayoi Iken (やよい軒) - Japanese sets. *Meals from 680 yen • 10am-11pm • Near Fukuro-machi*
Matsuya (松屋) - Rice bowls and curry. *Gyudon bowls from 290 yen • 24h • Kanayama-cho tram stop*
Nakau (なか卯) - Gyudon and curry. *Bowls from 290 yen. • 24h • Kanayama-cho tram stop*

Honke-kamadoya Bento (本家かまどや) - Cheap bento takeaway shop. *Bento boxes from 300 yen • Temmacho tram stop • 10am-5pm*
Hotto Motto (ほっともっと) - Bento boxes. *Bentos from 390 yen • 9am-10pm • From Hiroshima station north exit, head over the car park and bus stop area, then up the road with the Lawson convenience store (near Hiroshima Bank)*
Hokka Hokka Tei (ほっかほっか亭) - Bento boxes. *Bentos from 399 yen • 9am-10pm • Shukkeien-Mae tram stop*

Cheap supermarkets (スーパー)

MaxValu (マックスバリュ) has a store on the north side of the station (6am-12am). Head past the car park and bus terminal, and the supermarket is in the building with Hiroshima Bank (広島銀行 広島駅北口支店 in Japanese, if you are lost). There is also one in Sogo department store, near Kamiyacho-Nishi tram stop (10am-9pm).

Shopping

Seria (セリア) - Two locations of the 100 yen shop chain, one in the Sogo department store near Kamiyacho-Nishi and the other in the Fukuya department store outside the south exit of Hiroshima station. *10am-8pm*

Recommended cheap accommodation

Hostels and guest houses

Backpackers Hostel K's House Hiroshima
Japanese hostel chain with good prices and many happy customers! Eight-minute walk from Hiroshima station. *Dorms from 2600 yen •* http://kshouse.jp/hiroshima-e/

J-Hoppers Hiroshima Guesthouse
Friendly hostel with a variety of dorms and private rooms, based in an old ryokan (Japanese hotel) building. Next to the Peace Park. *Dorms from 2500 yen •* http://hiroshima.j-hoppers.com/

Capsule hotels

Capsule Hotel Cube Hiroshima
Right outside Kanayama-cho tram stop, a walkable distance from the main sites. It has free wifi, clean capsules and female-only areas. *Capsules from 2700 yen*

Internet cafes

Aprecio (アプレシオ)
Modern internet cafe with a host of seating plans, showers and wifi. Free drinks, as per usual! *Night packs (ナイトパック) available from 6pm: 9 hours (9 時間パック) 2000 yen, 12 hours (12 時間) 2200 yen • Near Hiroshima station south exit, in the amusement complex opposite the post office (5F)*

How to get there and away

By rail

If you have a rail pass, take the Shinkansen, otherwise prices are crazily high for such a journey, and the bus is the better option. The Shinkansen takes 4.5 hours from Tokyo, 90 minutes from Osaka (Shin-Osaka) and 100 minutes from Kyoto. *Recommended rail passes: Japan Rail Pass, Kansai-Hiroshima Area Pass, Kansai WIDE Area Pass*

By bus

Hiroshima is on major bus routes, such as from Tokyo (12 hours, from 6450 yen) or Osaka (6 hours, from 3500 yen) with Willer Bus or JR Bus. Changes may be required in Osaka if coming from the north. *Recommended bus pass: Japan Bus Pass*

Tourist information (観光案内所)

There are three information centers in Hiroshima station. One is in the underground section from the south exit (9am-7pm), another is just at the south exit (9am-5:30pm) and a final one is on the Shinkansen side (9am-5:30pm).

Miyajima (厳島)

Miyajima is yet another UNESCO World Heritage site near Osaka and Hiroshima. One of Japan's most popular areas, it offers an easy to access and peaceful rest from the big city. Everything on the island is within walking distance, so it's a great spot for budget travelers.

Discount pass: Visit Hiroshima Tourist Pass

If you are not using a Japan Rail Pass, or a regional pass, then this pass is a great option, and will at least save you a few dollars. Allows unlimited use of Hiroshima Electric Railway Lines (which can also be used to access Miyajima Guchi station) and the ferry to Miyajima, as well as local buses for three days. Also includes a booklet of discount coupons to various attractions and shops in the area. Available from Hiroshima station (south exit information desk). *Small Pass 1000 yen (Hiroshima city and Miyajima), Wide Pass 3000 yen (includes areas around Hiroshima)*

Things to do

Itsukushima Shrine (厳島神社)

Now a World Heritage site, this 1400-year-old shrine complex is built out over the sea. The stand-out style and bold architecture sets this shrine apart from the rest. The combination of forest greenery in the background, Otorii Gate in the distance and the unique structure make for an ultimate photo taking experience. *Adults 300 yen (+ Treasure Hall 500 yen), children 200 yen (300 yen) • 8am-5pm • Near Otorii Gate*

Otorii Gate (大鳥居)

The icon of Miyajima, this huge red torii gate looks like it's floating in the sea. It was built 200 meters out to sea, at a height of 17 meters. Come here at 5am-6am to walk under it in low tide, then later in the day to get a photo of it partly submerged in water. *FREE • 24h • 10-minute walk south of the ferry terminal*

Itsukushima Shrine Town (厳島門前町)

Full of old-fashioned shops and inns, this town dates back as far as the Kamakura period (1185–1333). Life changes slowly in these parts, and the old town still retains a laid back atmosphere with its family businesses. Tourists now bring in the main income for those that live here. *Few minutes south of ferry terminal*

Daisho-in Temple (大聖院)

Located at the beginning of the Daisho-in Route up the mountain, this amazing temple complex is skipped by many, but is definitely worth the short walk from town. It used to be one of the most prominent before the Meiji period, so there are lots of historical features to admire. *FREE • 8am-5pm • 5-minute walk south of Itsukushima Shrine*

Senjokaku Hall (千畳閣)

Also known as Hokoku Shrine, this large wooden hall takes its name from its incredible size, as 'Sen' means 1000 and 'jo' means tatami mats, so it's approximately the size of 1000 tatami mats! The shrine was built for chanting Buddhist sutras for fallen soldiers. There is also a small pagoda. *100 yen • 8:30am-4:30pm • Just north across road from Itsukushima Shrine, to the north*

Miyajima History and Folk Museum (宮島歴史民俗資料館)

This museum is located in the former home and storehouse of the Egami family, a once wealthy merchant family on the island. It has some interesting displays about the lives of people on the island over the years and some paintings of spots across the island. Also has a surprisingly large wooden spoon, so a good spot for selfie enthusiasts! *Adults 300 yen, children 150-170 yen • 8:30am-5pm (closed Mondays and New Year holidays) • 2-minute walk west of Itsukushima Shrine*

Hiking up Mount Misen

No need to take the expensive cable car, as there are three well signposted, easy hiking routes up the mountain. A great view greets visitors once they get to the top, but walking through the virgin forest is just as enjoyable.

Momiji Dani Route

Takes visitors along the Momiji River, which in autumn is especially beautiful with the golden leaves of the momiji trees, past some oddly shaped rocks and some interesting plant life. Gets quite steep on the second half. *Difficulty: Medium • Hike time: 90 minutes to 2 hours*

Daisho-in Route

With more than 2000 stone steps up to the summit, this hike up is better for less experienced hikers. Takinomiya Shrine and Shiraito Fall are also interesting spots along the way. *Difficulty: Easy • Hike time: 2 hours*

Omoto Route
The more challenging of the routes, this one takes hikers through Omoto Park, full of fir trees, before entering Komaga Forest, the second largest forest on the island. Also has a huge rock named Fuji Rock and Iwaya Taisha shrine. *Difficulty: Medium • Hike time: 2 hours and 30 minutes*

Budget food

Expect tourist prices here, so budget travelers should bring over food from the mainland. If you want to eat out, the old town has some traditional Japanese restaurants, with prices from around 700 to 1100 yen. Basics such as soba, curry rice and ramen are available. There are also a few stalls selling snacks from 200-400 yen, so worth trying some new bites.

Cheap supermarkets (スーパー)
There is no large supermarket on the island. While there are convenience stores around the ferry terminal on the mainland, there is also a Fresh Box supermarket (フレッシュボックス) a short walk away (9am-8pm). From Miyajima Guchi station, walk down to the right at the main exit, then cross over at the first rail crossing. Take a left, then walk down on the left for a minute or so.

Recommended cheap accommodation

Miyajima Guest House Mikuniya
We stayed here on our first trip to Miyajima and found the rooms to be large and clean. Great for large groups and centrally located near Itsukushima Shrine. *Dorm beds from 4000 yen* • http://miyajimamikuniya.com/

Backpackers Miyajima
A cheaper option, this hostel is back on the mainland, but super close to the ferry terminal. Friendly staff are eager to help travelers. *Dorm bed from 2900 yen* • http://www.backpackers-miyajima.com/en/

How to get there and away

From Hiroshima station, take the Dentetsu tram to Miyajima Guchi station (69 mins, 270 yen). If using a Rail Pass, take the JR **Sanyo Line** to Miyajima Guchi station (27 mins, 400 yen without pass). From Miyajima Guchi station, walk to the ferry terminal. Take one of the frequent ferries to Miyajima (10 mins, adults 170 yen, children 80 yen). If you have a Japan Rail Pass, use the JR ferry (free). *Recommended rail passes: Japan Rail Pass, Kansai-Hiroshima Area Pass*

Tourist information (観光案内所)

Inside Miyajima ferry terminal (9am-6pm).

Himeji (姫路)

Himeji is most famous for its castle, which became a World Heritage site in 1995. It's worth visiting along the route from Osaka to Hiroshima just for this castle, considered the best in Japan.

Discount pass

Get a combined Himeji Castle and Kokoen Garden pass for 1040 yen, just 40 yen more than the castle ticket. Can be purchased from either location.

Things to do

Castle area

Himeji Castle (姫路城)

A real must-see if you are in Japan, Himeji Castle was first constructed 400 years ago. The recent rebuilding has been done very authentically, and the structure really towers over the city, being called the "white heron castle". Everyone you meet who has been here will say it's the grandest castle in Japan. Sitting on a highly elevated platform, Himeji Castle is a huge complex surrounded by some pretty gardens, so it's also great for the cherry blossom season. *Adults 1000 yen, children 300 yen • 9am-5pm, until 6pm Apr 27 - Aug 31 (closed New Year holidays) •* http://www.himejicastle.jp/en/

Kokoen Garden (好古園)

Until 1992 unopened to the public, this is a Japanese garden located right next to the castle, offering nine unique gardens divided by traditional fortress-like walls, which were constructed using the ruins of the Himeji Castle West Mansion and surrounding samurai residences. It was constructed at the site of the old lord's residence and is often used for period dramas. *Adults 300 yen, children 150 yen • 9am-5pm, until 6pm Apr 27 - Aug 31 (closed New Year holidays)*

Walk it and save!

You can access the two main attractions on foot. It's an easy 15-minute walk up the shopping street north of the station. Otherwise use the Himeji Castle Sightseeing loop bus from Himeji station (100 yen, day pass 300 yen).

Volunteer guides and tours

Himeji Castle English Speaking Guide Group - http://www.i-guide.jpn.org/
Local tour group provides tours around this city, as well as the castle, for a few hours. Contact a few weeks before you arrive.

Volunteer Guide Association of Himeji Castle
Free tours of the castle and Kokoen Garden, usually available every day. Tours can be joined at the guides office near the ticket office.

Mount Shosha (書写山)

This is a 371-meter tall mountain near Himeji, the top of which is full of Buddhist temples of the Tendai sect. The most famous is Shoshazan Engyō-ji (書寫山圓教寺), which is often used when filming historical movies and dramas due to its authenticity and total lack of modern blemishes. Mount Shosha offers an excellent chance to get up in the mountains for just an afternoon or a slow day. Transportation is cheap and easy, plus there is lots to see once you get up there, with all the countless Buddhist temples, small shops and of course vending machines! *Difficulty: Medium (easy with ropeway) • Time required: 3-4 hours (half with ropeway)*

Hike and save!

Walk to the left behind the cable car station, and you will see an English sign pointing to the walking route up the mountain. Later on some signs are just in Japanese (look for 登山道 and follow the red arrows). Just before you enter the forest, you will see a "Gun hunting prohibited" sign with another sign on the right side, with arrows pointing left and "0.8km" written. Turn left and start your mountain hike up! *Small donation required just before summit. Ropeway: One-way adults 500 yen, children 250 yen. Return ticket: Adults 900 yen, children 450 yen (From 8:30am-5pm to 7pm, check at tourist information center in Himeji station before departing) • From Himeji station bus stop no.10, get the bus to Mount Shosha (30 mins, 270 yen)*

Budget food

Miyuki Street (みゆき通り)

While there are some convenience stores and a few restaurants on the main road up to the castle, the main street to head for food is definitely Miyuki Street (Miyuki Dori). From the east exit, it's the street with the blue and yellow Matsumoto Kiyoshi pharmacy (look for the Japanese characters). Here are a few highlights, if walking from Himeji station.

Iyoseimen (伊予製麺) - Basic Japanese sets, but specializing in soba. *Sets from 500 yen • 5th block on right*

Kimura Taiyaki (木村家のたいやき) - Taiyaki (fish shaped sponge cake with fillings). *Taiyaki from 150 yen • 7th block on right*

Negidako Genten (元天ねぎ蛸) - Takoyaki (octopus balls) takeout joint. *Takoyaki plate from 600 yen • 8th block on left*

Cheap supermarkets (スーパー)

Pantry & Lucky is a supermarket in the station (10am-9pm), while a larger supermarket called MaxValu is in the Terasso shopping mall (マックスバリュテラ ッソ), a short walk down the road on right side from the east exit (7am-midnight). There is also a Bon Marche supermarket (8am-9pm) next to the Daiso 100 yen store mentioned below. Prices are cheaper for the ones outside the station.

Water bottle refill spots

Some water fountains are available around the castle complex.

Shopping

100 yen shops

Daiso (ダイソー) - Opposite exit 2 of Sanyo Himeji station, next to the main JR station. *10am-9pm*

Seria (セリア) - Inside Terasso shopping mall (same as MaxValu supermarket). *10am-9pm*

Pharmacy (ドラッグストア)

Matsumoto Kiyoshi (マツモトキヨシ) has a pharmacy across from Himeji station, east exit.

Recommended cheap accommodation

Himeji 588 Guesthouse

A friendly guesthouse with a large communal eating area, and walking distance from the castle. *Dorms from 2700 •* http://himeji588.com/eng/

Kaikatsu (快活 CLUB 姫路駅前店)

Free ice cream, drinks and a variety of seats and booths at this net cafe, plus a women-only area. Showers are charged extra. *8 hour night pack (8 時間ナイト) 1543 yen • Second block on right, on main road from Himeji station east exit*

How to get there and away

By rail

If you have a JR rail pass, from Kyoto (45 mins), Shin-Osaka (30 mins) or Tokyo station (3 hours), take the Shinkansen to Himeji station. Otherwise take a rapid train. From Osaka station, take a JR Special Rapid to Himeji station (1,490 yen, 1 hour). From Kyoto station, first take the JR Special Rapid Service to Osaka station first, then the above train (2,270 yen, 90 mins to Himeji). *Recommended rail passes: Japan Rail Pass, Kansai Area Passes, Kansai-Hiroshima Area Pass, Kansai Thru Pass*

By bus
Shinkibus provides services from Osaka and Kyoto stations (from around 2000 yen), available from the bus terminals at these train stations, but trains are much easier and often cheaper. From further afield places such as Tokyo, getting an overnight bus with Willer Express or JR Bus is much cheaper than a train. Prices from Tokyo start from around 4000 yen. *Recommended bus pass: Japan Bus Pass*

Tourist information (観光案内所)
Inside Himeji station (9am-7pm).

Okayama (岡山)

Korakuen Garden

Large city in Chugoku, known across the country for Korakuen Garden, a superb example of Japanese gardening. It's worth stopping off here for a morning or an afternoon if traveling between Hiroshima and Kyoto.

Discount pass
Pick up a Combined Ticket for the garden and castle when visiting them, for 560 yen, saving 140 yen. Enough to buy a strange Japanese drink at one of the vending machines nearby!

Things to do

Korakuen Garden (岡山後楽園)

One of the three most celebrated traditional Japanese gardens in the country, this 300-year-old site has beautifully manicured lawns with hills and interwinding lanes, tea houses, plus Japanese ponds, tea plantations and lakes. What sets it apart from most Japanese gardens is the grand, wide lawns and the Enyo-tei House, the former living quarters of the lords who used to own the land back in the 17th century. *400 yen • 7:30am-6pm (Mar 20 - Sept), 8am-5pm (Oct - Mar 19) • 5 mins walk from Shiroshita tram stop*

Okayama Castle (岡山城)

This six-storey reconstructed black castle shows off many fascinating relics, but it is not the most visually stunning castle in Japan, so quite skippable if you are visiting others. Having said that, it is still officially considered one of the top 100 in Japan. Visitors can dress up for free as feudal lords or princesses inside, so it's a fun, cheap alternative to other castles. *Adults 300 yen, children 120 yen • 9am-5:30pm (closed Dec 29-31) • 5 mins walk from Shiroshita tram stop*

Yumeji Art Museum

Popular museum featuring the works of Okayama poet and artist Yumeji Takehisa from the early 1900s. Takehisa was known for creating the "Bijin-ga" style, a way of portraying women using S-shaped lines to show off their beauty. *Adults 700 yen, children 400 yen • 9am-5pm (closed Mondays, New Year holidays) • Just over the river from Korakuen Garden •* http://yumeji-art-museum.com/

Okayama Orient Museum (岡山市立オリエント美術館)

Modeled after the Pantheon in Greece, this museum displays more than 3000 pieces of oriental art. Good spot if you have some time left, but far from essential. *300 yen • 9am-5pm (closed Mondays) • Next to Shiroshita tram stop*

Walk it and save!

Although there is a tram network in Okayama, the main sites are only half an hour or so on foot from the main station. Just head out the east exit, and down the main, wide road heading away from the station.

Budget food

Budget restaurants

Hakata Ikkosha (博多一幸舎) - Hakata style tonkotsu (pork based) ramen. *Ramen from 790 yen • Inside Okayama station • 11am-11pm*
Yoshinoya (吉野家) - Gyudon and curry. *Bowls from 330 yen • 2nd block up main road from east exit, on right side • 24h*
Sukiya (すき家) - Gyudon and curry. *Bowls from 360 yen • Okayama station • 24h*
Yayoi Iken (やよい軒) - Japanese sets. *Meals from 680 yen • Okayama station • 7am-11pm*

Cheap supermarkets (スーパー)

Yours Supermarket (ユアーズ) is located on the east side of Okayama station (7am-10pm). There is also one in Aeon Mall, south of the station at exits 6 and 7 (7am-10pm). The nearest one to the garden is Fresh Marche (フレッシュ・マルシェ), located south of Shiroshita tram stop (9am-8pm).

Shopping

Daiso (ダイソー) – 100 yen shop, located in the Aeon shopping mall to the south of Okayama station (exits 6 +7). *10am-9pm*

Pharmacy (ドラッグストア)

There are two Matsumoto Kiyoshi pharmacies (マツモトキヨシ) in Okayama station (8:30am-10pm).

Recommended cheap accommodation

Most people tend to continue on after Okayama, or stay in Kurashiki, which has a host of cheap hostels. But there are a few good options if it's more convenient to stay here:

Sauna and Capsule Hotel Hollywood

Right outside the station, this cheap capsule hotel (men only) does the job. Clean, quiet and English signs to help those not familiar with capsule hotels or Japanese spas. *Capsules from 2700 yen*

Comic Buster (コミックバスター)

Net and comic cafe chain. Free drinks bar available, plus there are cheap meals for a few bucks. Showers 300 yen. *Night packs (ナイトパック): 6 hours (6 時間ナイトパック) 1630 yen, 10 hours (10 時間ナイトパック) 2140 yen • One block down the main road from the east exit, on right side*

How to get there and away

By rail

If you have a rail pass, take the Shinkansen, otherwise prices are crazily high for such a journey. The Shinkansen takes 4 hours from Tokyo, 1 hour from Osaka and 70 minutes from Kyoto. *Recommended rail passes: Japan Rail Pass, Kansai-Hiroshima Area Pass, Kansai WIDE Area Pass*

By bus

Okayama is on major bus routes, such as from Tokyo (10 hours, 5000 yen) or Osaka (from 3500 yen, 3 hours) with Japan Bus Lines or JR Bus. *Recommended bus pass: Japan Bus Pass*

Tourist information (観光案内所)

Inside Okayama station (9am-6pm, closed New Year holidays).

Kurashiki (倉敷)

Possibly Japan's most picturesque merchant town, which lines a lovely canal, dating back to the Edo period. The town was taken over by the Shogun leaders 300 years ago and converted into a trade center for the rulers. It still retains the charm of these early years, with almost all the buildings in the historic area begging for a picture to be taken. The area has some interesting museums, cafes and restaurants to experience, most of which are housed in tastefully converted merchant buildings.

Walk it and save!
Walk to the canal area, which has all the below tourist spots. It's only 10 minutes or so on foot from the station. If you don't want to spend lots of money on museums, it's perfectly possible to spend a day walking around the area. Be sure to head off down some of the less trodden traditional streets that go off from the main canal or shopping streets and take a stroll.

Things to do

Kurashiki Bikan Historical Quarter
All the below spots are well signposted, with plenty of tourist-friendly street maps to help you out. But as mentioned, the best way to experience this town, especially for budget travelers, is just to walk around and pick up a few interesting Japanese snacks as you go around.

Kurushiki Museum of Folkcraft (倉敷民藝館)
Three Edo-period rice granaries, dating from the late Edo period (1603–1868), have been converted into this museum about folkcraft in Japan. Around 4000 folkcraft objects are on display, including ceramics, rugs, bamboo items and other textiles.
700 yen • 9am-5pm (Mar - Nov), 9am-4:15 (Dec - Feb) (closed Monday and Dec 29 - Jan 1)

Japanese Rural Toy Museum (日本郷土玩具館)

Edo period house now open to the public, with more than 5000 old-school and rural toys from all over the Japan, from as far back as the Edo period. Very kitsch museum, so worth a visit if you want to try something a little different. *400 yen • 9am-5pm*

Ivy Square (アイビースクエア)

Built in the center of a former cotton mill, this square is full of hip cafes and restaurants. There is a small memorial museum and a few interesting souvenir shops. *FREE • 24h*

Archaeological Museum (倉敷考古館)

This former storehouse exhibits more than 1400 relics unearthed in the surrounding Chugoku region, plus some from south America. Housed in a whitewashed storehouse, the exhibits range from prehistoric stone implements to ancient bronze bells. *400 yen • 9am-5pm (March - Nov), 9am-4:15pm (Dec - Feb) (closed Monday and Tuesday apart from national holidays, and Dec 29 - Jan 2)*

Honmachi-Higashimachi Street (本町踊り、東町踊り)

A quiet, nostalgic street full of old tradesmen's homes. These were mainly constructed in the Meiji era (17th to 20th centuries) and are now shops, mini museums and inns. *3 min walk from Ivy Square*

Volunteer guides and tours

Kurashiki Goodwill Guides - GWG_kurashiki@kurashiki-v.net
Tours around the Kurashiki Bikan area, available in English, Korean and Chinese. The tours take visitors to the highlights of this small town. Advance booking required.

Budget food

Inside Ario Kurashiki shopping mall (outside the north exit) there is a Ringer Hut (リンガーハット) for fish based ramen from 630 yen, Katsu Don (かつ丼) for rice bowls from 490 yen, plus other reasonably priced food court stalls. There are few budget chain restaurants here if you want to eat out, so best to go the mall if you don't come across something more to your liking.

Cheap supermarkets (スーパー)

Tenmaya Supermarket (天満屋) is located on the lower level of Ario Kurashiki shopping mall (9am-9pm).

100 yen shops

Can Do (キャンドゥイ) - One in the South Station shopping mall attached to Kurashiki station and another in Ario Kurashiki shopping mall (9am-9pm).

Recommended cheap accommodation

Kurashiki no Guesthouse Kakure-Yado Yuji-inn

Friendly new guesthouse with helpful staff, a large living room to meet new people and share travel ideas and traditional Japanese rooms. Free tea and coffee. *Dorm beds from 3500 •* http://yuji-inn.com/

172

Kurashiki Youth Hostel
Little bit of a walk from the action, but this well run hostel has some of the best prices in town and the official YHA stamp. *Dorm beds from 3024 yen*

How to get there and away

By rail
From Okayama station, take a JR **Sanyo line** train to Kurashiki station (15 mins, 320 yen). *Recommended rail passes: Japan Rail Pass, Kansai-Hiroshima Area Pass, Kansai WIDE Area Pass*

By bus
Kurashiki is on most bus routes, such as from Tokyo (10 hours, 6000-8000 yen) or Osaka (from 3500 yen, 3-4 hours) with Willer Bus, Japan Bus Lines or JR Bus. *Recommended bus pass: Japan Bus Pass*

Tourist information (観光案内所)

One is inside the station (9am-6pm Oct - March, 9am-7pm Apr - Sep) and another in the Kurashiki Bikan Historical Quarter (9am-6pm).

Bitchu-Takahashi (備中高梁)

A real surprise, this has to be one of the most fascinating castles towns we have ever visited. While Bitchu-Takahashi is a small town not on most tourist maps, it has a scattering of fascinating and traditional relics and architecture, plus a beautiful castle hidden on top of a small mountain. Part of the charm of the town is that it really isn't too well geared up for tourists. While it has a tourist information office for help, we only saw one other tiny group of foreign travelers. The rest were a few elderly Japanese travelers challenging the walk up to the castle. Worth a day trip if you are heading to/from Hiroshima or Okayama on the Japan Rail Pass.

Discount pass: Combination Ticket

It's highly recommended to buy the combination ticket for 900 yen. It provides access to all the local tourist spots in the area, including the ones listed below. You'll save a few bucks on the main tourist spots, plus it includes some nice shrines and museums that you may otherwise skip because of entry costs. It also includes a handy map. Available at the tourist information center.

Things to do

Walk it and save!
Bitchu-Takahashi is all done on foot, so is great for budget travelers. English signs around town show where to go, and there are lots of sights, such as the shrines and museums included in the combination ticket, along the way to keep you entertained.

Bitchu Matsuyama Castle (備中松山城)

Officially one of Japan's top 100 castles, once you get up there you will be amazed to see how quiet it is. There were never more than a dozen people when we were there. Built in 1250, it's classed as an Important Cultural Property of Japan and located at the top of a mountain 430 meters up. There is also a temple complex a little further on from the castle, and some great views over the mountains. Our favorite castle in Japan, mainly due to how authentic and unspoiled it is. *Time required: 3 hours return, Difficulty: Easy in town, medium going up mountain • 300 yen • 9am-6pm*

Takahashi Old Town

Take a stroll around the old town with your Combination Ticket. You really need to get the combination ticket to enjoy it all in a day, otherwise you will be spending a bit too much for some of the rather small tourist spots here. If you are really short on money or time though, you could just go straight up to the castle.

Raikyu-ji Temple (頼久寺)

Zen temple with a history that goes back several centuries. The temple is surrounded by a lovingly crafted garden, with helpful staff ready to help answer any questions. *Adults 300 yen, children 200 yen • 9am-5pm*

Takahashi Museum of History

A quaint old museum, which seems to be set in some old school building. Full of all kinds of antiques and odd pieces from the past few centuries in Japan. A nice mix, from 1970s electronics to old wooden carts. A good spot to escape from the tourist trail and see something a little different. *300 yen • 9am-5pm*

Budget food

It's a small town here, so probably best to head to a convenience store. There is a Lawson convenience store outside the west exit of the station, just to the right, plus a 7-Eleven further up the road. Both have a large selection of takeout meals.

Cheap supermarkets (スーパー)

Head up the wide road heading out from the west exit to reach Sakae Supermarket (サカエ), on the right at the end of the first block (9am-6pm).

Polka Happy Town (ポルカ天満屋ハピータウン)

Continue down the main road past Sakae Supermarket, then take the first left at the next traffic light and walk down for 10 minutes. Polka Happy Town has a Daiso 100 Yen shop (10am-9pm), a Little Mermaid bakery (10am-6pm) with bread from 129 yen and a ramen restaurant (11am-9pm) with bowls from 660 yen.

Water bottle refill spots

Bring plenty of water, or buy some cheap drinks before at the above supermarket before heading up to the castle. As this is Japan, there are vending machines on the way, but you can save a bit by buying your drinks at the supermarket.

How to get there and away

If using a rail pass, from Okayama take a limited express train to Bitchu-Takahashi station (35 mins). Otherwise, take a local train on the JR Hakubi Line to Bitchu-Takahashi station (50 mins, 840 yen). *Recommended rail passes: Japan Rail Pass*

Tourist information (観光案内所)

There is a small tourist information center just up the main road from the west exit. A must visit before you begin (9am-5pm).

Shimanami Kaido (しまなみ海道)

This mega cycling route is becoming an increasingly popular, but still relatively quiet cycling route across the islands connecting the mainland and Shikoku island. The 60 kilometer route has been designed for cyclists in mind and the temperate climate helps to make the ride enjoyable and not too physically demanding. Along the way there are some eye-catching shrines, museums and some amazing sights over the sea.

Cycle and save!

Bicycles are available to pick up or drop off from terminals all along the route, so you don't need to do the whole route. The route is clearly signposted, with blue lines on the road showing the way and frequent multi-lingual maps. Pick up a free copy of the map when you rent your bike as well. Along the way, there are a few alternative routes, so see how you feel when you do it. Some say the route is tough, others have no problems.

Renting bikes

Renting a bike costs 1000 yen (children 300 yen), plus a 1000 yen deposit (children 500 yen), which is not returned if you drop off at a different spot. It's still best to drop off somewhere else though, as ferries often charge extra for carrying these back and you may miss the closing time on your return. From Onomichi, enquire at the tourist information center for rentals (rental park open 7am-7pm). Further spots for renting or dropping off are noted on the free maps given out there, or at http://www.go-shimanami.jp/global/english/bicycle/. Note that while the bridges over the islands are at time of writing toll free, this may change in the future.

Budget food and shops

Tourist centers along the way have restaurants, but they are quite overpriced. Along the main road, you will never be 10/15 minutes ride from the next convenience store, so best to get food at these, or bring your own. In Onomichi, there is an Aeon supermarket (イオン尾道店). To get there, head out of the north exit of Onomichi station, walk to the left to reach the bicycle park, then take the road on the right. Go up a few hundred meters until you get to the Aeon mall (7am-9pm).

Water bottle refill spots

Some of the tourist centers along the way have public water fountains, but budget travelers should buy a large bottle at the supermarket before heading off, or bring their own large bottle.

100 yen shops

Can Do (キャンドゥイ) - Located in the Aeon mall. *9am-9pm*

Free wifi locations

Free wifi is available at the tourist restaurants along the route.

How to get there and away

On Honshu (Japan's main island), cyclists start from Onomichi. You can also start from Imabari in Shikoku, going the opposite direction. At present, it's not advised to use the bridge over from Onomichi to the first island of Mukaishima. Instead of this, head to the ferry terminal to the south of the station and use the ferry to Mukaishima (110 yen).

With a Japan Rail Pass or other pass

From Osaka (90mins) or Kyoto (100 mins), take the Shinkansen to Fukuyama, then transfer to the **Sanyo Main Line** to Onomichi. Imabari is a limited express stop between Matsuyama and Okayama/Takamatsu.

Without a rail pass

Both Imabari and Onomichi are connected to highway bus networks. Local and express trains also stop at both.

Getting back on the bus or ferry

If you are ready to finish along the way and return back, there are a variety of bus and ferry services. Buses go all along the route, but a transfer may be required (2250 yen all the way). Double check latest times at the information centers before heading off. The ferry services are:

Onomichi Port – Shige Higashi Port – Sawa Port – Setoda Port
All the ports have bike terminals nearby. Only four boats per day stop at Sawa Port. *1050 yen (additional 300 yen for bicycle) • 40 minutes all the way • Departures every 1-2 hours*

Imabari Port – Tomoura Port – Kinoura Port – Habu Port
There is a cycling terminal near Habu Port. Additional fees for taking the bicycle, and a few ferries don't allow bikes (ask when you rent the bicycles for latest info). *1750 yen • 75 minutes • Departures about every 2 hours*

Tourist information (観光案内所)

There is a tourist information center in Onomichi. Pick up a cycle map from here if you would like, although there are maps and signs along the way.

Many thanks for reading

Help spread the word!

Please help us by writing a review on the website where you bought the book, sharing the book on Facebook or Twitter, or telling a friend. As this is a self-funded indie project, it would be super useful and very much appreciated! Arigatou!

Like or follow us to get the latest tips and deals

Join us on Facebook at https://www.facebook.com/supercheapjapan or follow us on Twitter at https://twitter.com/SuperCheapJapan to receive information on new discounts, latest deals and interesting budget travel reports. You can also join our newsletter for monthly roundups of this information at http://www.supercheapjapan.com/.

Picture Attribution

Ueno, Harajuku and Shibuya pictures ©Tokyo Convention & Visitors Bureau
Kinkakuji photo: ©Mr Hicks46, used under the Attribution-ShareAlike 2.0 Generic (CC BY-SA 2.0) license. Original file can be found at https://flic.kr/p/grWMnZ.
Mount Fuji photo: © Miles Root http://www.milesroot.com/

Found an error with this book? Please send us an email at supercheapjapan@gmail.com

About the Author

Super Cheap Japan was written by Matthew Baxter, a British travel author living in Tokyo, the heart of Japan. Having traveled across the country for several years, without much money, he has built up an extensive knowledge of budget travel in the Land of the Rising Sun. He now writes professionally for several websites and publications, such as the Japan National Tourist Association, Japan Visitor and All About Japan.